THE CRAFT OF
MUSICAL COMPOSITION

by

PAUL HINDEMITH

BOOK I
(FOURTH EDITION)
Theoretical Part

English Translation by
ARTHUR MENDEL

PRICE . . . $4.00

SCHOTT MUSIC CORP.
NEW YORK, N.Y.
Exclusive Distribution for the United States

Belwin Mills Publishing Corp.

CONTENTS

[v]

HINDEMITH

THE CRAFT OF MUSICAL COMPOSITION

Theoretical Part

CHAPTER I

Introductory

"Perhaps some will wonder at my undertaking to write about music, when there are at hand the opinions of so many excellent men who have written learnedly and sufficiently about it, and particularly at my doing so at a time when Music has become an almost arbitrary matter, and composers will no longer be bound by laws and rules, but avoid the names of School and Law as they would Death itself . . ."

Thus wrote Johann Joseph Fux in the foreword to his *Gradus ad Parnassum* (1725),* the textbook of counterpoint according to whose basic principles the student to this day still learns his craft. Now for us the first decades of the 18th century represent the fullest flowering of the technique of composition. When Fux's book was published, J. S. Bach was forty years old, and at the summit of his skill and creative power; and the minor masters who were to be found all over Europe exhibited even in works which were by no means heaven-storming a complete technical mastery. But Fux, the strict contrapuntist, whose field is vocal music, cannot reconcile himself to the shift of the center of the composer's work to the instrumental domain, with all that that shift implies for the style of writing. The step from the noble but narrowly limited art of writing for voices, in which instruments must always play a secondary rôle, toward freer and livelier tone-progressions

* *"Mirabuntur fortassis nonnulli, cùm tot præstantissimorum Virorum exstent monumenta, qui de Musica perquàm doctè, & abundanter scripserunt, cur ego ad hoc scribendi genus me contulerim, hoc maximè tempore, quo, Musicâ ferè arbitrariâ factâ, Compositores nullis præceptis, nullisque institutis obstringi volentes, Legum, ac Scholæ nomen ad mortis instar exhorrescunt; . . ."*

[1]

such as naturally occur to the gifted instrumentalist, appears to him not as the beginning of a path into a new land, but as a descent which must be halted. How in both word and deed he opposed what he considered the barbarization of music may be seen both in his compositions and—with explicit reference to the master of the purest and most perfect style of writing, Palestrina—in the *Gradus*.

Perhaps the craft of composition would really have fallen into decline if a genius like Bach had not fought his way through to the highest and most complete mastery of his material, and if Fux's *Gradus* had not put a brake upon caprice and exaggeration, and set up a standard of excellence in writing. For this was the first real textbook of composition in a time which had known on the one hand only the passing on from master to pupil of specific devices and tricks of the trade, or, on the other, deep-searching theoretical works that were of little help in learning the practical art of composition.

A musician who feels called upon in these times to contribute to the preservation and transmission of the craft of composition is, like Fux, on the defensive. He is, in fact, even more so than Fux, for in no other field of artistic activity has a period of over-development of materials and of their application been followed by such confusion as reigns in this one. We are constantly brought face to face with this confusion by a manner of writing which puts tones together according to no system except that dictated by pure whim, or that into which facile and misleading fingers draw the writer as they glide over the keys. Now something that cannot be understood by the analysis of a musician, making every conceivable allowance for individual characteristics, cannot possibly be more convincing to the naive listener. In *Die Meistersinger* one reads, it is true, that the composer must make his own rules and then follow them. But this privilege is granted only to a *master*—one, moreover, who knows, or at least feels, the bases of his work provided by Nature.

It is not surprising that things have developed as they have. The discovery, in the last century, of the extreme limits of power and subtlety in the effect of musical tone extended the boundaries of the tonal domain at the disposal of the composer into hitherto undreamed-of distances. New combinations of tones came to be recognized, and new ways of bending a melodic line were discovered. It seemed as if the sun had risen upon a new, glowing, iridescent land, into which our musician-discoverers rushed headlong. Blinded by the immense store of materials never used before, deafened by the fantastic novelty of sound, everyone seized without reflection at whatever he felt he could use. At this point instruction failed. Either it fell into the same frenzy as practice, and devoted itself to flimsy speculation, instead of adapting its systems of teaching to the new material, or it lapsed into inactivity, and what had never been a very strong urge towards novelty turned into a barren clinging to the past. Confidence in inherited methods vanished; they seemed barely adequate now to guide the beginner's first steps. Whoever wished to make any progress gave himself unreservedly to the New, neither helped nor hindered by theoretical instruction, which had simply become inadequate to the occasion.

2

A considerable portion of the responsibility for the failure of instruction belongs to the instructors themselves. Is it not strange that since Bach hardly any of the great composers have been outstanding teachers? One would expect every musician to have the desire to pass on to others what he had labored to acquire himself. Yet in the last century the teaching of composition was looked on as drudgery, as an obstacle in the way of creative activity. Only rarely did a composer integrate it as a component part of himself; the feeling of responsibility for future generations of musicians seemed to have become a thing of the past. Not until the last few decades do we again find composers who feel it their duty to educate pupils. These men act in the spirit of the old handicraftsmen, who aimed to hand on their skills intact. In times that boast of an enviable flowering of the craft of composition, great masters can afford to devote themselves exclusively to their own creations, paying no attention

[3]

to those who are to come after them. It is then the task of the teachers, who follow at a distance, to mint into current coin the wealth which the composers have mined. But today, when there is a general lack of skill in the technique of composition, no composer should withdraw from teaching.

There are two types of theorists: the teaching composer, and the avowed specialist in teaching musical theory. A gifted composer is not always a good teacher. But his instruction is bound to have a certain creative warmth, even when the composer is of modest gifts, because he is passing on directly what he himself has experienced. This is not true of the usual theory instruction, such as is given in most schools. The specialist who gives such instruction without himself being gifted for composition is in a difficult position. In the painful early stages of trying to bring dry series of figured basses and sets of rules to life, he cannot fall back upon his own creative activity. Thus he is likely to turn this most interesting of fields, which lies directly adjacent to that of free composition itself, into a morass of disappointment, instead of exploiting the many stimuli it offers for the better understanding of past and present styles of composition. Not every theory teacher can reach that high estate of knowledge and ability attained by the teachers (and textbook writers) of the last century, for they owed the richness of their harvest to the fact that composers had left the field of instruction to them. But he can at least prevent the theory lesson from becoming what students too often consider it: a boring, incomprehensible, and useless burden. And is it really any more than that when it consists in handing out "music" in the form of dead chord-progressions and monotonous, meaningless melodic lines?

The teacher must not base his instruction simply on the rules of textbooks. He must continually refresh and complete his knowledge from the practice of singing and playing. What he teaches must have been developed out of his own exercises in writing. For it is his task not only to teach the pupil a correct technique, but also to help him obtain a comprehensive musical education, seeing to it that his work in the practical fields is supplemented by an intelligent understanding of the theoretical side. It is up to him to pass on the most personal and most painfully arrived at secrets of the great composers, so that he may call forth in the student at least a small reflection of their light. At the same time, he must exercise a guiding and calming influence on the young musician who is in the throes of experiment; he must steer him between the Scylla of blind worship of the past and the Charybdis of idolatry of the present. Anyone who follows this profession for the sole purpose of earning his living is just as unworthy of it as is the (fortunately not too common) composer who submits unwillingly to what he considers the slavery of teaching, and poisons the student with his inevitable musical bad temper.

One thing that makes instruction in this field more difficult is the unfortunate fact of its division into two separate parts. Of course the material must be presented to the student in easily graspable form; exercises for the development of melodic invention must alternate with those for the acquisition of a cogent harmonic style, just as the student of an instrumental technique employs both finger exercises and pieces for performance in learning to master his instrument. But complete separation of the harmonic material, followed after a whole year of work by melodic studies which are themselves insufficient, is as thoroughly wrong as would be a method of skating in which one had to practise exercises for working each leg separately before one learned to move on the ice.

In Fux's time, it was possible to get along with the material he worked out. But when the technique of composition developed further, particularly on the harmonic side, the teaching of harmonic phenomena and their treatment was set off in a separate field known as Harmony. This took place about the beginning of the 19th century (although it was based upon much research of earlier times). In this procedure, the new progress in composition seemed to have found the educational method appropriate to it. But that method soon turned out to be inadequate, and after barely a hundred years of an apparently brilliant existence, the fabric, which from the beginning has needed patch after patch, is now worn threadbare. On the other hand, the Fux system has lasted two hundred years, and is still passed on from teacher to student almost in its original form

[5]

—a grotesque state of affairs when one realizes that the practice of composition has long since forsaken the bases of this system. This fabric was never patched; it was made of more durable stuff. In fact, the stuff was so durable that it might well have been ripped out and worked over again. But no successors came to adapt its basic principles to new needs. Some were for greater strictness, and stripped Fux of an ornament here and there; others added new spangles to the old garment. But the truth is that no matter what is done to make it more presentable, it no longer fits our needs, and the want of something more suited to our own problems has long been felt.

If, then, every music student must go through these two courses of study, adapting himself painfully at first to the one, only to be torn away from it before he is really used to it and then have to begin all over again on the other, finally to realize that even when he has mastered the new discipline he has acquired no real mastery over his tonal materials—is it any wonder that the idea should arise that a composer should not let himself be disturbed by what he has learned in his theory lessons?

It is in the nature of such a teaching procedure that in the case of an unusually gifted student there comes a day when the teacher can no longer follow the activities of his pupil. He does not understand what the student is aiming at—although in technical matters there can be no secrets—and, as is touchingly described in many biographies, he lets him depart with his blessing, since there is nothing more he can teach him. Unfortunately for the teacher, in most cases the pupil comes to this conclusion on his own account, and does not wait to be dismissed.

3

Because of the situation described above, it is a particularly difficult task today to give a student instruction in composition. One teacher sticks close to what he has had handed down to him. For him what Riemann or Prout said is iron-bound law. His pupil learns the old styles of writing: he can modulate, write counterpoint almost in his sleep, from the first species to the florid fifth, and construct fugues to order, made according to the text-book rules, and containing anything but music. If the precocious student seeks to know more, mentioning that in the music he plays and hears there is more to be discovered, he is hushed up, or given excuses, false explanations, or denials; or the teacher becomes angry; or relations between pupil and teacher are broken off altogether. Or, on the other hand, the teacher may let the pupil flounder around in a field in which both are lost. But none of these ways brings the pupil any nearer to his goal.

Among the younger teachers—who have themselves experienced the impact of the new music on their own work, and now wish to spare the pupil the things that once caused them pain, anger, and disappointment, without arming them for later struggles—many allow the pupil considerable freedom from the start. But freedom is a bad thing at the beginning, since it does not provide the student with the necessary support. A conscientious teacher, who can hardly justify to himself the process of continuing to dispense outworn materials, is in a perpetual state of uncertainty, since no usable new method is at his disposal. How, in particular, shall he treat the more advanced student? He can settle technical problems with him only by relying on nothing more substantial than his taste, citing his own opinion and that of other honest seekers, and exploring the situation with the student. None of these solutions will do except the last, and this can be fruitful only if the teacher and pupil are sympathetically attuned, and both of exceptional gifts. But no general system of instruction can be based on such a happy combination of circumstances.

If confusion in the technique of composition is not to increase and spread, if the conflicting results of an outworn system of instruction are not to bring disaster in the wake of uncertainty, a new and firm foundation must be constructed.

4

I propose to attempt the construction of such a foundation. I am not animated by any desire to freeze into permanent shape what I

[7]

have been teaching for years, either to get it out of my system or to be rid of the burden of continually improvising new forms of the material which I have often handed out. Anyone who has for years taught students who wish to know why the masters are free to do what is denied to them, why one theme is good and another poor, why harmonic progressions may be satisfactory or irritating, why sense and order must prevail even in the wildest turmoil of sounds, and why such order cannot be arrived at with the traditional tools; anyone who has not sidestepped this unending struggle with the Why of things, and, at the risk of laying himself bare before his pupils, has taken each new question as a stimulus to deeper and more searching study—anyone who has faced these issues, I say, will understand why I feel called upon to devote to the writing of a theoretical work the time and trouble which I would rather spend in composing living music.

I have experienced the needs of the teacher as well as the strivings of the composer. I have lived through the transition from conservative training to a new freedom perhaps more intensely than anyone else. The new land had to be explored if it was to be conquered, and everyone who took part in this process knows that it was not without danger. The path to knowledge was neither straight nor smooth. Yet today I feel that the new domain lies clearly spread out before our eyes, that we have penetrated the secrets of its organization. This was not accomplished by the stubbornness of those who simply put up a pretense of strength by persisting in their accustomed disorder, or by those who were so self-righteous that they never experienced temptation. Anyone who is familiar with the development of music after the first World War will find step by step in these pages, which are intended to afford entrance to the newly won territory, traces of struggle with external circumstances as well as of that inner strife whose aim is the perfection of one's own work. But even a wider circle of readers will understand, at this first stopping-place on the road to complete clarification of both contemplation and action, that an attempt to explain the music of the present day had to be undertaken, if only to satisfy a personal need to pass on to new learners what had been acquired by learning, and to shorten for them the paths which until now have been inevitably roundabout.

I address myself above all to the teacher. True, I cannot (as is understandable in the case of a composer whose theorizing is only incidental and enforced) offer him a book of rules, polished down to the last detail, in which he can simply assign to his pupils three pages per lesson. Perfection cannot be attained at the outset of an innovation such as the present one, and the comprehensive working out of the material presented here will require the efforts and the experience of many musicians. The teacher will find in this book basic principles of composition, derived from the natural characteristics of tones, and consequently valid for all periods. To the harmony and counterpoint he has already learned—which have been purely studies in the history of style: the one based on the vocal style of the 16th and 17th centuries, the other on the instrumental style of the 18th—he must now add a new technique, which, proceeding from the firm foundation of the laws of nature, will enable him to make expeditions into domains of composition which have not hitherto been open to orderly penetration.

To the composer, as well as the teacher, the book offers new perspectives on his materials, and makes clear that for a well-intentioned but arbitrary arrangement of sounds he must substitute an order which only to the uninitiated will seem a restriction of the creative process. In reality, wisely and sensibly directed work will result in greater variety than a profusion of over-seasoned or over-sweet progressions, the formula for which is soon transparent and thus available even to those who have no inner musical vocation.

The reader who lightly turns these pages in the hope of a stimulating general discussion will not be well rewarded. He will find the subject matter remote and dry, the more so as he is used to meeting the materials of music in living and flowering form, rather than on the dissecting table. Moreover, he finds more pleasure in the actual sound of music than in reading about it, and thus he may well leave the present accumulation of descriptions of abstract tone-successions, practical rules, and musical examples to those who can feel the pulse of music beneath the monotonous consideration of its materials.

Those industrious ones, too, who think that by memorizing and working hard at rules and precepts they will come by a recipe for producing convincing music had better give up the search. Finally, this book would represent a disappointment to the beginner who expected to find in it a reliable guide for self-instruction. It presupposes a considerable body of knowledge, and will therefore be valuable only to those who are already somewhat familiar with the technique of composition.

In the present Theoretical Part of this work, the underlying principles of the new theory are first established and then developed. I have limited myself to what is really new, and to that older material to which I give a new interpretation. Such elements of older theories as have remained intact throughout all periods and styles, because they are independent of period and style, I have left untouched, except where it has been more convenient to rename or reclassify them. Nothing is said here about those things which remain unchanged, or about the actual writing of music, with its rules for voice-leading, spacing, and so on. Book II, devoted to actual writing in two parts, contains all this material, both old and new, presented in pedagogic order.

In Fux's foreword, the following additional passage occurs:

> "The practice of medicine is intended for the sick, not for the well—although my work does not aim, and I do not lay claim to the power, to control the current of a gushing stream that has overflowed its banks, or to reconvert composers from their heretical way of writing. For aught I care, everyone may follow his own fancy." *

But despite Fux's modest estimate of his powers, he actually did do away with heresy. His "gushing stream" seems to us, compared

* *Ægrotantibus etenim, ac non bonâ valetudine gaudentibus medicina paratur. Quanquam labor meus non eò tendit, nec tantum mihi roboris arrogo, ut quasi torrenti extra limites præcipitanter erranti cursum inhibere, Compositoresque de licentiosa scribendi hæresi ad resipiscentiam revocare me posse confidam. Per me liceat cuique sequi suum consilium.*

with the torrential flood of today, a mere overflowing mountain brook. Perhaps a single man's strength will not suffice today to dam the flood; perhaps what he attempts will not even be understood, much less valued. Yet the success of Fux's work shall be a good omen for mine.

5

The reader who thinks that the views here expressed amount to a deification of materials, an undue exaggeration of the importance of mere craft, should remember that there was once a time when he had to absorb the rules of harmony, which, despite the limitations of the chordal material dealt with, were numerous enough. There is no denying the fact that to learn a new system takes time and trouble. But if one gains both a wider outlook and a more complete mastery, it is worth it. Technical skill can never be great enough. No one is too able or too accomplished to learn more than he knows. Technique must be learned as a child learns to move his limbs: what was difficult at first must become easy; it must be at one's instantaneous disposal; it must function so perfectly that its action is no longer noticed; it must sink to the level of subconscious activity.

Although the creative process in its highest stages may always remain hidden from human comprehension, as may the mysterious source of artistic work in general, yet the dividing point between conscious and unconscious work can be raised to an extraordinary degree. If this were not true, everyone in whom this point lies at a very low level could assert that he is creating the greatest works of art. There would be no difference between Beethoven and any other composer, who had with difficulty achieved a mere quarter, say, of the height of artistic achievement that men may attain, and knew nothing of the other three quarters that still lay above him. Such a little man would not care to speak of technical matters, but would instead refer to his impulse, his feeling, his heart, which had prescribed the way for him. But must not this impulse be tiny and this feeling negligible if they can express themselves with so little knowledge? Is not an immense mastery of the medium needed to translate into tones what the heart dictates? Can the inner vision of the music that the composer has glimpsed make itself at all clear to another if the resistance of the tones and the refractoriness of tonal progressions is continually coming between the impulse and its expression in sound?

The road from the head to the hand is a long one while one is still conscious of it. The man who does not so control his hand as to maintain it in unbroken contact with his thought does not know what composition is. (Nor does he whose well-routined hand runs along without any impulse or feeling behind it.) The goal must always be such mastery that technique does not obtrude itself, and a free path is prepared for thought and feeling. The man to whom the tones are a necessary evil with which he must wrestle; or who sees in them a perfectly tractable medium in which he can express himself without any restraint; or who climbs up on them as on a ladder, or wallows in them as in a bog—such a man is simply adding to the infinity of pieces that are written every year without moving a human ear or spirit. The initiated know that most of the music that is produced every day represents everything except the composer: memory, cheap compilation, mental indolence, habit, imitation, and above all the obstinacy of the tones themselves. Our principal task is to overcome the latter. To do this we need precise knowledge of the tones and of the forces that reside in them, free from aesthetic dogma and stylistic exercises such as have characterized previous methods of instruction, but leading the composer rather according to natural laws and technical experience.

In this attitude toward the technical side of composition I am in agreement with views which were held long before the classic masters. We find such views in early antiquity, and far-sighted composers of the Middle Ages and of modern times hold firmly to them and pass them on. What did tonal materials mean to the ancients? Intervals spoke to them of the first days of the creation of the world: mysterious as Number, of the same stuff as the basic concepts of time and space, the very dimensions of the audible as of the visible world, building stones of the universe, which, in their minds, was constructed in the same proportions as the overtone series, so that measure, music, and the cosmos inseparably merged. And the art of composition itself? To pious musicians it was a means of praising God, and of enabling the community of listeners to take part in that praise. That the work has been created to the glory of the Highest Being, of whose support it is thus assured, we can feel in the music of many composers—above all in that of Bach, whose "Jesu iuva" in his scores was for him no empty formula.

We cannot conjure up past times, although every man must come to some agreement with himself about the bases of his work. But that our consideration of tonal materials and its application by all who may concern themselves with it may catch a kindling spark from the spirit of the old masters is the hope from which this work springs.

CHAPTER II

The Medium

1

General Considerations

If we were to ask an intelligent musician, who knew his *métier* and who had a certain theoretical knowledge, what tones he would choose from among the audible range, what series he would consider the most natural, the simplest, and the most practical raw material for composition, he would undoubtedly reply after a moment's thought that we must mean a scale, for without a scale no ordered music would be conceivable. He would be thinking of the major and minor scales, which provide an inexhaustible supply of tones for all possible harmonic combinations, and according to which all melodies known to him can be classified. He would be forgetting, however, that our ancestors made use of other scales, and that even today peoples of other cultures use scales that often have little similarity to ours.

Even the simplest musical activity, uninfluenced by education or experience—the song of the savage, or the first attempts to draw tones out of a hollow bone or a reed pipe—must make use of some interval-progressions which are based fundamentally on a series of adjacent tones. The primitive musician, giving direct expression to his mood, will at first not be interested in the exact distance of one tone from another. Not until considerable experience has broadened his knowledge and raised the level of his desires will he feel the need of bringing order into the luxuriant tonal wilderness.

It will then develop that certain intervals make similar impressions upon all men. When even the man of the lowest level of civilization hears the interval of an octave, he will feel that the upper note is the higher image of the lower. Accordingly, in all known tonal systems, the basic scale-patterns, with few exceptions, fill in the space between two tones an octave apart.

After the octave, the next fixed point to be felt is the fifth. But the conception of this interval as something fixed and unchangeable is for the untrained ear a more difficult matter. The two tones do not merge completely into one sound, as do those of the octave. The upper tone is not felt, as is the upper tone of the octave, to be the mere higher duplication of the lower. Nevertheless, the interval of the pure fifth is so unambiguous and independent that it is to be found in almost every scale system. Other intervals (thirds, sixths, sevenths, and seconds) are less easily determined. The distance between the two tones of a major sixth, for example, can be diminished or augmented to a certain extent without destroying the impression of a major sixth. The slightest alteration in the size of an octave or a fifth, on the other hand, changes these intervals completely, so that the ear perceives them only as greatly expanded sevenths and fourths or greatly contracted ninths and sixths.

2

Overtones

We find the intervals embedded in the tonal raw material which Nature has made ready for musical use, consisting of an infinite number of tones, from the deepest barely perceptible drone to the whistle that lies at the other limit of audibility. Into this inchoate tonal mass we can introduce a certain order by the use of the immutable measures of the octave and the fifth. Nature, in fact, has herself introduced this order, and put at our disposal a whole series of other intervals as well.

The eye perceives in light which has been split up by a prism a natural series of vibration frequencies. The light of the sun always produces the same immutable series of colors, familiar to us in the rainbow. Now, just as light consists of graduated colors of the

[15]

spectrum, so a tone consists of many partial tones. The spectrum of the world of sound is the harmonic or overtone series. A tone produced by a voice or instrument carries with it a greater or lesser number of barely audible overtones. Their order is not arbitrary: it is determined by a strict law, and is as immutable as the color series of the rainbow. The series extends theoretically to infinite heights, but in practice a sounding tone is supported by only a limited number of overtones. It is well that this is so, for a tone accompanied by all the possible overtones, to the upper limit of audibility, would be obscured by their profusion, would lose its character, and would suffocate. Bells of poor quality, with their great number of prominent overtones, give us an idea of what such an overloaded tone would be like. For theirs is a chaos of tones, rather than a single tone, and as such it is of almost no use for musical purposes.

A tone completely devoid of overtones, on the other hand, is characterless. It has no profile; no expression. It cannot be produced on our musical instruments. A completely pure tone of this sort can be produced only electrically by means of an oscillator or similar apparatus. It is of virtually no musical value. Even tones which are relatively poor in overtones are not used in practical music, as the almost pure tones of tuning forks show. The soft, insipid tones of recorders of medium register, for example, or of the similar labial pipes of the organ, are of good effect only in combination with sharper tone-colors (*i. e.*, those richer in overtones). Our musical instruments, of which the larynx is one, produce their tone by the joint action of vibrating solid bodies, which in turn cause the air to vibrate. All the vibrating parts of the instrument possess one or more tones proper to them, as we can observe by tapping the wood of the violin or the brass of the trumpet. Such tones are inseparably connected with the principal tone produced by the instrument. Even if the latter were free of overtones, the tones proper to the material of which the instrument is made would be heard along with it.

The overtones accordingly have an important relation to tone-color. The latter depends not only on the nature of the material and construction of the instrument producing it, but also on the manner in which its vibrations are excited: the articulation, the manner of drawing the bow, the touch, all have an important influence on the distribution of the overtones. Every tone-color corresponds to a certain grouping of the overtones. The ear hardly hears them separately; it only perceives the disappearance of some or the addition of others as changes in tone-color.

3

Nature of the Overtone Series

In order to study the nature and construction of the overtone series, we shall take the structure based on the fundamental tone C as the basis of our observations:

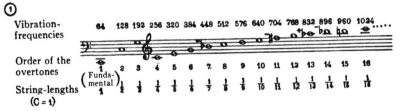

We know that this fundamental tone supports a series consisting of the octave, the fifth of the octave, a second octave, the major third of the latter, the octave of the earlier fifth, and so on, as illustrated by Fig. 1. The spaces between the individual overtones thus grow progressively smaller, in arithmetical series. If we assume a frequency of 64 vibrations per second for the fundamental tone C (a convenient and usual basis for reckoning, even though the C actually used in our music nowadays is somewhat higher—i. e., has a somewhat faster vibration rate)—then the second tone of the series will vibrate 128 times per second, the third 192, and similarly each tone will have 64 more vibrations per second than its predecessor in the series. The octave has twice as many vibrations as the fundamental, the twelfth three times as many, the double octave four times.

[17]

Octaves

The air-vibrations upon whose duration the duration of a tone depends, whose wave-length determines its pitch, whose amplitude governs its intensity, and whose shape gives rise to its color, are in turn dependent for their dimensions upon the size and period of motion of the vibrating solid body which produces them. To find out about the form and tempo of the vibrations, we must examine the body which generates them. The most useful such body is the string. If we stretch a string over a sounding board, and provide it with a sliding bridge, we have the ideal instrument for measuring tone—the monochord, which has been used by musical theorists since antiquity.

To produce the octave of the tone proper to the whole length of the string—that is, to double its vibration rate—we must place the bridge exactly in the middle, so as to divide the string into two equal parts. Half of the string-length vibrates twice as fast as the whole; one third vibrates three times as fast, and so on:

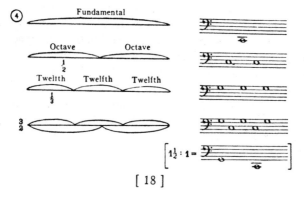

[18]

On both sides of the bridge which has been placed in the middle of the string we hear the octave of the tone produced by the whole string. If we wish to compare the string-lengths and the pitch-relationships of the two tones of this octave interval, we may imagine two monochord strings of the same measurements, of which one vibrates as a whole and the other in two halves. The two tones an octave apart are then related as 1 (1 string-length) to 2 (2 equal divisions of the string-length), written 1:2. If the string be divided into thirds, each third produces the twelfth of the tone of the whole string. The interval of a fifth may thus be expressed 3:2. One string is divided into 3 equal parts (and accordingly produces in each of its parts the tone g, assuming the tone of the whole string to be C); the other is divided into two halves (each producing c); and the difference is the perfect fifth (c-g). Or, in terms of the overtone series: the interval of a fifth is produced by the second and third overtones.* (Accordingly, the fifth between the fundamental C and the G above it, since it lies an octave lower and would be produced by string-lengths twice as great, would have to be expressed $\frac{3}{2}:\frac{2}{2} = 1\frac{1}{2}:1$.) If we continue to subdivide the string, we arrive at the proportions 4:3 for the fourth, 5:4 for the major third, 6:5 for the minor third, 5:3 for the major sixth, 8:5 for the minor sixth, and so on for all the intervals which occur in the overtone series.

The strings of stringed instruments offer a true parallel to the monochord when they are used to produce harmonics:

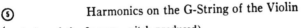

Harmonics on the G-String of the Violin

(o = placing of the finger; ♦ = pitch produced)

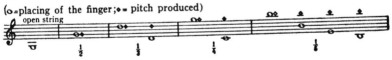

The lightly placed finger here replaces the bridge of the monochord, for the string is free to vibrate on both sides of this dividing point—which is not true in the case of the normally produced tone,

* It is customary to call the fundamental *number 1* of the overtone series; this makes the octave *number 2*, the twelfth *number 3*, and so on.

[19]

in which the part of the string which lies below the stopping finger is excluded from the production of tone—and the partial tones correspond exactly to those of the monochord, and consequently to the overtone series. The division into halves produces the octave, into thirds the twelfth, into fourths the double octave, etc.

The nature of the overtone series may also be easily observed in wind instruments. Those brass instruments which are so-called "natural" instruments (e. g., the bugle, post horn, hunting horn, Alp horn) sound the overtones of their fundamental, although only a small part of the series is used. The use of valves makes possible the addition of extra lengths to the tube, so that the ranges of the instruments are extended at the bottom.

ⓖ   Effect of the Valves of the B♭ Trumpet

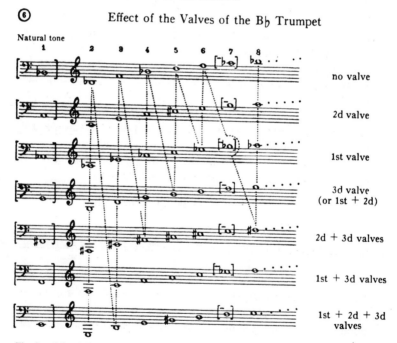

The dotted line indicates the best fingering of the chromatic scale.

Upon each of the tones thus added there rises the overtone series proper to it. The new overtones thus gained serve to fill in the gaps between the overtones produced by the original, unaltered tube, and thus make possible the playing of a scale. In trombones, the length of the tube is increased directly, by sliding part of it out, instead of by valves.

On our present-day brass instruments, players can reach about the 10th overtone, and on the lower instruments they can play some still higher in the series. Woodwind instruments, on the other hand, are confined to the first three or four overtones, produced, as on the brass instruments, by more intense blowing ("overblowing", sometimes with the help of the so-called octave keys).

⑦   Overblowing on the (Boehm) Flute

Quarter-notes indicate the fundamental tones which, when overblown, produce the pitches indicated above them.

*) somewhat flat
**) combination fingerings of two fundamental tones (overtone relations of 4:1 and 3:1)

The scale is here arrived at not by lengthening but by shortening the tube. To fill in the gaps between the tones of the overtone series produced by the whole tube, holes are opened which prevent the air from penetrating to the further end of the tube. The air column is thus shortened, it vibrates correspondingly faster, and creates new and higher fundamental tones whose overtones are also produced by overblowing.

[21]

4

The Triad

Tones 1–6 of the overtone series (comprising the octave, fifth, fourth, and major and minor thirds)

with their higher octaves (the two-fold, four-fold, and eight-fold multiples of their order-numbers, frequencies, and proportions) outline the extended major triad, which is to the trained and the naive listener alike one of the most impressive phenomena of nature, simple and elemental as rain, snow, and wind. Music, as long as it exists, will always take its departure from the major triad and return to it. The musician cannot escape it any more than the painter his primary colors, or the architect his three dimensions. In composition, the triad or its direct extensions can never be avoided for more than a short time without completely confusing the listener. If the whim of an architect should produce a building in which all those parts which are normally vertical and horizontal (the floors, the walls, and the ceilings) were at an oblique angle, a visitor would not tarry long in this perhaps "interesting" but useless structure. It is the force of gravity, and no will of ours, that makes us adjust ourselves horizontally and vertically. In the world of tones, the triad corresponds to the force of gravity. It serves as our constant guiding point, our unit of measure, and our goal, even in those sections of compositions which avoid it.

Must not then a music which consists exclusively of triads provide the highest delight? Pieces of this description, such as those of early Italian choral music, do not, as a matter of fact, belong among the greatest revelations; their uninterrupted sweetness is apt to bore even the gentlest listener. Hence a master like Palestrina sees to it that in his works the slight tension that resides in continuous triad successions is increased many times by melodic means, by suspended and passing tones, and thus a real tonal ebb and flow

[22]

is created even in the absence of passionate outbursts. Our aural nerves, as the result of the intensity of modern life and the surfeit of sounds, are very taut. Our ears take pleasure in music of a low degree of tension as a historical phenomenon, just as our eyes enjoy the quiet beauty of early painting. But of contemporary music they expect sterner emotions. They not only can stand passages without triads, they actually demand them. How great the span can be between triads is a question of the hearing habits of the listener and of the ingenuity of the composer. But from all the evidence it would appear that there is in the ear itself, apart from all questions of habit and ingenuity, a certain limit of irritability which it does not seem advisable to exceed by means of a music too far removed from nature—that is, from the triad. The awkwardness of a composer who cannot put together a convincing series of sounds, and the over-intelligence which, for fear of the commonplace, will not put a single triad on paper—both preclude any feeling of oneness with the work of art just as does the slanting floor of the "interesting" architect.

The feeling for the purity, the harmonic completeness, and the satisfying effect of the triad, which is the same as the unerring judgement in the aural measuring of the octave and the fifth, is accordingly just as natural to us as the body's sense of space. It is based on the nature of the ear itself. The senses of sight and feeling need to make use of memory and comparison in order to arrive at even approximate judgements of size and proportion, and our sense of the passage of time similarly does not permit us to make exact estimates. The ear, on the other hand, is the one sense organ that is unerring in its sense of measurement and proportion. The eye is like a mirror that reports faithfully and distinterestedly on what is before it. But the ear is like a fabulous sieve, that not only sorts what it receives into large and small, but measures it exactly. It hears simple ratios as beautiful and correct sounds, and it recognizes perfectly that the purity of the octave, the fifth, or the fourth is clouded when the proportions of length or vibration frequency are not in the ratios of $1:2$, $2:3$, or $3:4$. In the Cortian organ it literally possesses a minute frequency meter, each tiniest part of which is

[23]

attuned to a certain vibration rate, and responds to a certain wavelength. When vibration combinations in the simple ratios of 1:2, 2:3, or 3:4 strike this organ, they excite particular parts of its harmoniously designed structure, which distills from the feeling of correctness the most intense pleasure. This basic fact of our hearing process reveals to us how closely related are number and beauty, mathematics and art.

The seventh overtone in the series based upon C (–b♭¹) does not make the triad into a dominant seventh chord such as we know in practice. It is flatter than the b♭ that we are used to hearing as the seventh of c. Why we do not use the natural ratio 1:7 (or rather, 4:7) will be explained later.

Like the seventh overtone, the higher prime-numbered members of the series and their multiples do not fit into our tonal system. They also are either too flat or too sharp (indicated in our illustrations by the signs – or +)—although we must remember that it is only for simplicity's sake that we can let that statement stand. The natural tones of the overtone series cannot of course be "too sharp" or "too flat" in themselves. It is just that our tonal system, which strives to bring incomprehensible multiplicity within our grasp, cannot find any simple and clear place for them. In acoustical reckoning, so far as it serves as a basis for considerations of composition, one does not need these prime numbers, or the "pure" tones which lie above the 16th in the overtone series. No theory of music that is to be taken seriously has ever gone beyond the series 1–16, and we shall see in the course of our investigations that an even smaller portion of this series suffices to represent all the tonal relations used in music.

5

Paths to Scale-Formation

The overtone series in its raw state is not usable for musical purposes, on account of the constantly decreasing distance between its adjacent tones. For the melodic endeavor that has been known to man from time immemorial, in the simplest form of musical ac-

[24]

tivity—singing—, series of tones are needed to guide into definite channels what would otherwise be the arbitrary wandering of the voice. The intervals used for this purpose may be measured in various ways. But however they are arrived at, they must be small enough so that the progression from a tone to an adjacent tone is felt as a step and not a skip, if the series which they form is to be the basis for intelligible melodies. And in the series there must be an easily discernible order.

In contrast to the scales of oriental peoples, as well as to those of mediaeval Europe, our series will not serve exclusively melodic purposes. Not every scale that was originally evolved for melodic purposes is well adapted to the needs of harmonic organization. If a scale is to perform both functions, the intervals must be such that the combinations of tones are as pure as possible (that is, consist of intervals such as are contained in the lower reaches of the overtone series). On the other hand, the grouping of the intervals must not be so rigid that it does not permit of all those little divergences that form one of the greatest charms of melodic expression: the age-old use of impure intonation as an artistic means, the most extreme instance being the purposeful mistuning of subordinate tones in the melody, and the most minute divergence from the pitch being the vibrato, with countless melodic subtleties between these two extremes.

A prerequisite for the construction of a usable scale is the division of the entire tonal supply into fairly large sections of equal range, lying one above the other, each section filled out with the tones of the scale. That these sections have always begun with the octave of a tone taken as the point of departure is, as we have seen, only natural, given the facts of sound and hearing. Other divisions, such as the tetrachord system of the ancient Greeks, based on the fourth, or some scales of Arabian music which avoid the octave, are artificial structures, taking little heed of the overtone structure, and do not adapt themselves to our purpose. A system without the octave which would nevertheless be equally adaptable for harmonic and melodic purposes is conceivable, but it would be too clumsy for practical use. It would not even fulfill the requirement that must be met by a system designed for polyphony: the possibility of having two lines proceed in parallel motion. Even the simplest music will not always, it is true, move in parallel motion; yet the possibility of occasional parallels must not be limited to a few parts of the scale: it must be present everywhere. (The organum of the Middle Ages is only a preliminary step towards true polyphony; in the strict form of the uninterrupted coupling of voices it was rather the object of investigation by theorists than a type of living music.)

The next most important interval after the octave, the fifth, opposes considerable resistance to continuous parallel motion. As we shall see later, the uninterrupted connection of perfect fifths destroys the purity of the octave. But we cannot give up so important an interval altogether, and therefore we adopt it as the central pillar of our scale. With it we adopt the fourth, which is of course only the octave transposition of a fifth below the original tone.

Every octave will be filled out in exactly the same way as every other, so all we need is the scale pattern for one octave. In the following pages, the octave C-c is chosen as the range of the scale. To fill in the spaces between the first tone and the fourth, and between the fifth tone and the octave, there are several possible procedures. One of them seems to be indicated by the overtone series itself, for between the 8th and 16th overtones there is a scale-like formation

which contains the octave and the fifth, but not the fourth. On a wind instrument that can produce this series of the overtones of its fundamental, the 11th overtone, which is too high for the pure fourth, can easily be lowered by altering the embouchure, and the other tones can be similarly altered to fit. This practice was actually current for a long period; the so-called *"Klarinblasen"* on the trumpet, which existed up to Bach's time, was nothing else. But the continual tempering of the tones results, especially in fast tempi, in a good deal of uncertainty, and it is effective only in this one

[26]

octave, since the overtones in the octave below do not form a continuous scale, and since not more than the first two or three tones of the octave above are attainable by human lips and lungs. This series of tones has been of importance in musical practice, but never in musical theory.

Another method is more productive. It, too, goes back to earliest experience in instrument-playing, for it takes its departure from the fingerboard of stringed instruments. The innate tonal sense will lead the primitive player almost always to tune two adjacent strings in fifths or fourths; only after considerable harmonic experience are other intervals used for tuning. Now when he wishes to climb up from one open string to another a fifth or a fourth above, filling in the intervening space finger by finger—that is, stepwise—he will divide this space either according to the convenient placing of his fingers, or according to mathematical considerations. If he then transfers the divisions thus found to the next higher string (and to others still higher) he has achieved a usable scale. The Arabian tonal system, with its highly developed theory of music, rests on such calculations. Scales so arrived at are admirable material for monophonic music, purely melodic in conception, while for polyphonic music they are practical only to a limited extent, since for the sake of identical fingering on all strings—carrying with it the possibility of parallel motion throughout—purity is neglected. The intervals formed by the tones of the scale do not all have the same proportions as their prototypes in the overtone series. But in polyphonic music, the measuring ear continually seeks the pure intervals of the overtone series, and is dissatisfied not to find them. And to the extent that scales of this sort do contain pure intervals besides the fourths and fifths, their immovable rigidity prevents any free harmonic development. Polyphonic music demands that the tones may at any time be able to change their tonal significance, by relating themselves to changing roots (either of chords or of overtone series). A tone that has, for example, already served as a third must be able to become root, fifth, or seventh in succeeding chords. It is, however, impossible, as we shall see, for one tone to perform all these functions without change of pitch. Thus

[27]

either the purity of nature must be disregarded or the pitches must be movable, which would take away from this type of scale its most characteristic feature.

6

Tempered Tuning

There is no solution of the scale riddle that can reconcile these opposite necessities. Purity must be neglected or the possibility of unhindered polyphony sacrificed. It is thus astonishing that one of the most inspired inventions of the human spirit should have been arrived at by the space-dividing method just described: the chromatic scale in equal temperament, such as we know on our keyboard instruments. It, too, is necessarily a compromise, but the sort of compromise represented in commerce by the use of money in place of barter. The small change of music, the twelve-tone series of the equally tempered scale, has become the musician's universal medium of exchange. Except for the octave, not a single one of its intervals is exactly equal to a pure interval of the overtone series; even the fifth sacrifices something of its value. But the difference is just big enough for the ear to perceive it without being disturbed by it in polyphony.

At the same time, the ear is subject to a certain danger in being exposed only to music constructed of tempered intervals; it accustoms itself to their clouded qualities, and like a jaded palate loses its sense of natural relations. Fortunately, however, the instruments and voices which can produce pure intervals are in a majority over the keyboard instruments, and we need hardly assume that musical sensitivity will ever sink so low as to allow keyboard instruments undisputed mastery. Yet their advantages are invaluable. Apart from their special tonal effect, it is they that first made possible to us full and unimpeded mastery over the entire tonal domain. But the fact that practical music makes a distinction between keyboard and other instruments (although the distinction is not very sharp) testifies to our realization of the fundamental irreconcilability of the two. Compared with orchestra

[28]

music, or chamber music for strings or winds or combinations of the two, the literature in which the piano or organ is combined on an equal footing with other types is not very large. More often the keyboard instrument is subordinated, as in the piano accompaniment to a song; or it is contrasted as a solo instrument with the body of the others, as in the concerto for piano or organ. A sensitive string player will always find greater pleasure in chamber music for strings alone than in music with piano, and the latter seems the less pleasant, the more stringed instruments are set against the piano. In piano quartets and quintets, the group of instruments capable of pure intonation holds the balance even against the tempered instrument. Adjustments of the movable tuning to the fixed, which can be made in smaller combinations, are hardly possible in such groups. That is why this field of music, which shows the discrepancy at its most striking, has been little cultivated, even to the present day. The pitches of a single instrument capable of pure intonation, on the other hand, are easily adapted to the piano (which "gives the pitch") although mostly without the player's being conscious of the fact. Thus works for such combinations are numerous: they offer the composer the advantage of covering a great deal of harmonic ground with only two players.

7

Earlier Attempts at Scale-Formation

In our discussion of "Klarinblasen" (the use of the upper overtones of the trumpet) we saw that the direct taking over of the "scale" in the fourth octave of the overtone series does not lead to a satisfactory result. Even the use of tones from still higher portions of the series would not help, unless a selection were to be made from among the latter, and they were all to be transposed down five or six octaves to the same register. But such a selection, in the absence of any suggestion from the nature of the overtone series, could be only a matter of individual taste; and if one is to proceed arbitrarily one has no need of handling such refractory material as the upper reaches of the overtone series.

Attempts were accordingly made in early times to derive laws for scale-formation from the proportion of the simplest intervals, that is, from the lower portions of the overtone series. One well-thought-out system was devised in ancient Greece: the Pythagorean. It requires that a fifth (the ratio 2:3 of the overtone series) be established on either side of a given tone. This results in the above-mentioned establishment of the fifth and fourth as the back-bone of the scale. The fifth below the given tone is transposed up an octave to give the fourth within the octave in which the scale is to be constructed. The ratio 1:2, which, being the first interval of the overtone series, has priority over all the others, does not produce any new tones in such calculations, but simply enables us to transpose already existing tones, and thus makes it possible for us to gather within the space of one octave tones which were originally far apart. Above the fifth C-G and below the fifth F_1-C let us now construct another pair of fifths; this procedure can be continued as far as one wishes. But it need not be continued very far. For any seven-tone section of such a series of fifths will yield, when its widespread tones are gathered close together by means of octave transposition, a seven-tone scale made up of whole-tone and half-tone steps which will answer many requirements.

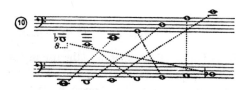

We can arrive at approximately the same result if we apply the interval originally existing between the fourth and the fifth—the major second—above and below each of our original four tones: the given tone, fourth, fifth, and octave. Such a scale includes tones, however, that do not form intervals corresponding to those of the natural series. Thus in the seven-tone Pythagorean scale starting from C with 64 vibrations per second, the E is too high:

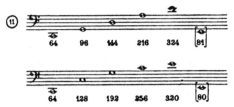

This is owing to the downward transposition of the fourth fifth above C, the e¹ with 324 vibrations, which is four vibrations higher than the fifth overtone of C (e¹ with 320 vibrations). This very striking discrepancy in so important an interval as the third (the "syntonic comma") makes the Pythagorean scale unusable for polyphonic music.

Now if one continues indefinitely adding fifths in an upward direction (setting up the circle of fifths), one is headed for infinity, for with the twelfth fifth a tone is reached which is also a comma higher than the octave of the original tone:

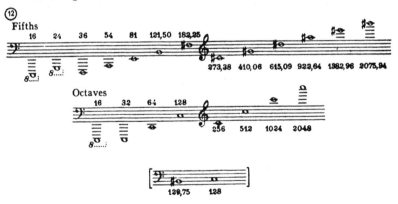

The next octave of the scale would have to be based on this tone (transposed down), which would be too high, and each succeeding octave would begin correspondingly too high. Thus the connection with the given tone would be lost. The ear is easily reconciled to impure fifths, if the discrepancy is very slight, as the equally tempered scale shows; but it would not accept impure octaves.

[31]

In order to avoid the disadvantages of this reckoning in pure fifths, the ratio 4:5 was introduced into the calculations: that is, the scale was no longer erected by superposing fifths only, but by the use of pure fifths in combination with major thirds. (We need not consider the ratio 3:4, of course, since the superposition of fourths would simply arrive by the opposite method at the same result as that of fifths.)

The scale thus arrived at offers the greatest number of intermediate tones of pure intonation; the third, particularly, now corresponds to the natural third. Although the remainder in the reckoning cannot be done away with, but must always obtrude itself in an impure interval, it is here at least not allowed to cloud the octave or any of the other most important intervals. Just as in one's home one places an unwanted object in some dark, out-of-the-way corner, so the comma is now placed in an interval that is not often used. Thus if C is the given tone, it will be least disturbing if the minor second or the augmented fourth is made the victim. The D♭ or the F♯ is then so out of tune that it cannot be used in an important place. Before the introduction of equal temperament, which took place during Bach's lifetime, keyboard instruments were tuned according to this system. Many varieties of the system were suggested, differing fundamentally only in the placing of the bad tone.

Anyone with a good ear who knows nothing of these things will be very much surprised by his experiences in trying to tune a piano. He will tend to be guided by his ear, joining one pure fifth to another; and by the accumulation of pure intervals he will go so far astray that in the end he will have achieved by great pains a tuning at least as bad as that he originally set out to remedy.

8

New Proposal

I now suggest a new method * for erecting a scale, which will lead us to goals that could not be attained by the method above

* See the table opposite page 48.

described. From what has been said, it is evident that I shall neither conjure away the comma nor suggest new structures of tempered series. I shall simply follow the suggestions which to the understanding ear lie hidden in the overtone series, and shall thus arrive at a simple and natural construction of the scale.

Construction by means of series of fifths and thirds does not represent a primeval method of erecting a scale. One is simply taking the scale already present in practical music and trying to explain the intervals of the series, which have already demonstrated their usefulness. What other reason would there be for the quite arbitrary ordering of the fifths and thirds? Or for the setting up of intervals like the Pythagorean third, which have so little correspondence with anything in nature? A more rational procedure gives up the attempt to measure every interval with the same unit.

Let us imagine ourselves back in the time of the creation of our tonal building materials. We know at this point only the single tone. We discover above it the overtone series, and feel our way gropingly up it, step by step. When we come to know the second tone of the series, we can learn something about it by comparing it with the original tone. When we come to the third, we have already had the experience of two, and with each succeeding overtone the possibilities of comparison increase.

We start again from the C that has 64 vibrations per second. From the second tone, the c with 128 vibrations, we cannot draw any important conclusions. If we give it the same rights that accrue to its progenitor, C, by virtue of the latter's place at the root of its overtone series, then c (128) becomes the fundamental of a new series, which reproduces the first series an octave higher, but without other change. We thus take it as the upper limit of our scale.

Let us now consider the third overtone, g, in the light of our knowledge of the two earlier tones. We could assign to it, too, the rôle of the first tone. It would then serve as the fundamental of a new overtone series, but as such, it would lie outside the octave C-c which we have set ourselves as the space within which we wish to erect our scale. But if we take this g as the second tone of an overtone series (that is, assign to it the rôle played by the c in the first series), it becomes the octave of a fundamental, to which it is related as 2:1. To arrive at this new fundamental, we divide the frequency of the g (192) by 2:

The result is G (96). We may thus adopt the following rule for our procedure:

> *To arrive at each new tone of the scale, divide the vibration-number of each overtone successively by the order-numbers of the preceding tones in the series.*

This formula gives us the key to all the remaining calculations. Anyone who has followed the path which we have taken from C through g to G will have no difficulty in understanding the origin of our tonal planetary system.

Let us apply the measures already discovered to the next overtone of C, namely c^1 (256). If we take it as the upper tone of the relation 2:1, we obtain, by halving its vibration-number, a tone we already have, c (128). But if we take the c^1 as the third overtone of a series—if we assume that it bears a relation to a fundamental like that of the g to the C (3:1)—we shall divide the vibration-number of the c^1 (256) by 3, and obtain the tone F (85.33):

We treat the fifth overtone, e^1 (320), similarly. As the upper tone of the ratio 2:1 it belongs to the fundamental e, a tone which lies outside the octave we wish to fill in, and is accordingly of no use to us. But if we treat it as the third overtone, and divide its frequency by 3, we obtain A (106.66). And if we treat it as the fourth overtone, we obtain E (80):

[34]

The g¹ (sixth overtone, 384), if treated as the second overtone, yields a tone (g, 192) which lies outside our octave. As the third, it yields the c which we already have as the second overtone of C. As the fourth, it again yields only a tone which we already have—the G. But by dividing it by 5 we obtain an addition to our series—E♭ (76.8).

The seventh overtone is a special case, as we shall see. It thus draws a boundary-line above the six tones already considered. Let us then, before proceeding to its consideration, subject the first six overtones to a still closer scrutiny. Up to this point, we have treated each one as if it stood one or more places *lower* in the overtone series than it actually does. Now let us adopt the opposite path. This is a procedure of the second order. It is not based upon the experience which we gather step by step in going from one tone to the next, and which accordingly permits us to use at each new level only the relations which lie below it. Rather, it uses the sum of the experiences gathered in attaining the levels reached thus far (up to and including the sixth overtone), in that it considers the relations into which each successive tone of the original series could enter if it were considered to lie *higher* in a series (but not higher than the sixth overtone). This is no arbitrary procedure. Having set the upper limit of our calculations at the sixth overtone (because of the special nature of the seventh), and having treated each overtone with the measures of those preceding it in the series, there is no other way to arrive at new scale-tones except to apply to each of these overtones all the other proportions.

The third overtone, g, may thus be taken as the fourth, fifth, and sixth overtones of new series:

The fundamental tones of these series add nothing to what we already have. The G_1 (48) which results from dividing 192 by 4 is already represented by its octave, G (96); likewise the $E\flat_1$ (38.4), produced by the division by 5. Finally, division by 6 produces only C_1 (32), of which the octave is the C (64) with which we started. We cannot, of course, change the scale-tones which we have achieved through our calculations (and which, be it noted, are now to be considered fundamentals, not overtones). But upward transposition by an octave constitutes an exception to that statement, since it produces nothing new except the second overtone, which is already present, in sound as well as in theory, and which can therefore belong to our scale just as much as its fundamental.

The frequency 256, belonging to the fourth overtone, c^1, is now to be divided by 5 and by 6:

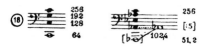

We thus arrive at $A\flat_1$ (51.2) whose octave (102.4) will fit into our scale, and F_1 (42.66), which is already represented by its octave (85.33).

The fifth overtone, e^1 (320), treated as the sixth, and its frequency accordingly divided by 6, produces the lower octave of the A which we already have:

[36]

9

The Seventh Overtone

The seventh overtone of C, –b♭¹ (448), cannot be used. If we attempted to apply the same procedures to it as to its predecessors, we should arrive at terrifying results. According to these procedures, we should have to consider it in succession a second, third, fourth, fifth, and sixth overtone. This would produce:

–b♭ (224), which lies above the limits of our octave; –e♭ which is unusable for the same reason; –B♭ (112) of which we may say in advance that it suits our purposes less well than the B♭ (113.78) which we shall arrive at by other means. (The superiority of the latter will appear from the consideration of the distances between the tones, which we shall soon undertake.) We should also achieve a –G♭ (89.6) that suffers from the same disadvantage as the –B♭, and finally an –E♭ (74.66) which would cloud the E♭ (76.8) already present in our scale.

In the distances between the tones, there must be some clear order. The smallest interval thus far is the minor second between E and F, and it should not be hard to establish this as the smallest interval in our scale. But the new smallest interval –E♭ (74.66) to E♭ (76.8) would assert its claims. And since it would not do to provide only one or two tones of the scale with auxiliary tones which were simply slight flattenings of the original tones, every tone of the scale would have to be provided with a similar auxiliary.

[37]

And these auxiliaries would have to have other tones at a similar distance below them, and so on, until we should have a hundred or more separate tones to the octave. Such a structure would be impractical, and instrumental technique could not cope with it. To realize to the fullest extent how meaningless it must remain for practical music, one need only imagine a singer hopelessly struggling with such small intervals.

In the play of harmonic intervals—that is, in chord-progressions—every tone of the scale must be capable of being used not only as a root but also as any other factor of a chord. To this rule the tones derived from the seventh overtone could be no exception. And every one of them would support an overtone series of which the seventh overtone must be treated like the seventh of the original series. The result would be chaos.

Is it not remarkable that musical mankind, after thousands of years of musical practice, should not have arrived at mastery of the characteristics of the seventh overtone? Attempts to include it in our tonal system have not been lacking. And, like other "impure" tones, it can of course be introduced melodically, if it performs a clearly subordinate function in filling out the main spaces. But its introduction into harmonic practice would have the results described. The attempt to expand our system in this direction is just as futile as it would be to try to make fractions instead of whole numbers the basis of our reckoning. Numbers and number-relations meant more to antiquity than they do to us, for we have lost the sense of the mystery of number through our familiarity with price-lists, statistics, and balance sheets. The secret of the number 7 was well known; to conquer it was to become the master or the destroyer of the world. It is understandable that such a mystic and unfathomable number should have been looked upon as holy. And in the world of tone, too, we must acknowledge the holy circle to be inaccessible.

10

Derivation of the Remaining Tones

The overtones lying above the seventh cannot be used for the derivation of further scale-tones, any more than the seventh one itself. In the course of such use, each one would have to serve once as seventh overtone, and thus the tonal tangle produced the first time would be made infinitely worse. But our scale is not yet complete, even though we have examined the realm of the six overtones from all sides.

The generative power of the parent tone, C, is exhausted. The tones c, G, F, A, E, E♭, and A♭ surround it like a proud group of sons. They will begin to lead lives of their own only when· they leave their father's house. This process in the family of tones is called modulation. But they can establish their own households while they are still under the protection of their father, and can present their progenitor with a throng of grandchildren. What this means is that we must treat those overtones of the tones G to A♭ which lie within the compass of the first six overtones of C (C-g¹), in the same way as we treated the original overtones. As the method is now familiar, only brief explanations will be needed.

The third overtone of G, d¹ (288) (3 × 96) gives us, when its frequency is divided by 4, D (72):

With this we may compare the D that is produced by dividing the ninth overtone of C, d², by 8:

We may further, by dividing this same d¹ by 5, derive B♭₁ (57.6):

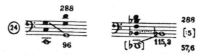

The upper octave of this tone (the tone itself lies below the octave of our scale) is B♭ (115.2), which is not suited to our scale, for the distance between it and the adjacent A (106.66) would be disproportionately large. What was said above about −E♭ (74.66) thus applies to this B♭, in the opposite sense. The next overtone of the G produces only tones which we already have, for it is the same as the sixth overtone of C.

The third overtone of F corresponds to the fourth of C, and accordingly is of no further use to us. But the f¹ (341.33) on the other hand, the fourth overtone of F (4 × 85.33), gives us something we did not have before, B♭ (113.78), arrived at by dividing the f¹ (341.33) by 3:

Dividing this same f¹ (341.33) by 5 we get D♭ (68.27):

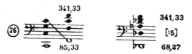

The overtones of A (a and e¹) do not produce anything new.

From the E, by dividing its third overtone b (240) by 2, we derive B (120):

The late-born sons E♭ and A♭ provide us with the tones G♭ (92.16), c♭ (122.88) and F♭ (81.92). But we shall not accept these gifts. We shall find the G♭ elsewhere, in a better form, at the desired distance from its neighbors (that of the half-tone E-F);

[40]

the c♮ (122.88) disturbs the earlier grandchild B (120), and the F♮ (81.92) does not agree with the E (80). In the course of chord-progressions, these tones may occur, either through modulation, in which the relation with the C series is suspended, or, while still related to the C, as mere neighbors of B♭ and E♭, or otherwise in a harmonically subordinate rôle, so that they have no independent existence.

And now the sons of C have done their duty, and still our scale is not complete. If we arrange the tones in upward succession from C to c, we encounter a gap between F and G. The distance between every other pair of adjacent tones is a half-tone.

We can complete the family by including in it the great-grandchildren of C. The grandchild B♭ (113.78) produces a G♭ (91.02), through the division by 5 of its second overtone b♭ (227.56):

We may obtain the same tone from the D♭:

The fourth overtone of this D♭, d♭¹ (273.08), divided by 3, gives a G♭ (91.03), whose insignificant fraction, like that of the G♭ (91.02), we may disregard. But the two grandchildren D and B also have offspring. The fifth overtone of the D, which is the same as the third overtone of the B (namely f♯¹), divided by 4, gives an F♯ (90), having one vibration less than its related G♭:

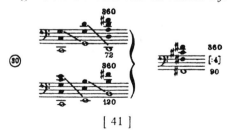

[41]

We apparently have here, in the relation of F♯ to G♭, what we sought to avoid in our consideration of the seventh overtone: an excessively small distance between two tones of the scale. But this is true only in this one instance, and the other tones of the scale are not affected. We can accommodate ourselves to this slight disturbing factor, whereas we should have had no defense against the *Götterdämmerung* of the tones which the fatal seventh overtone would have initiated. A comma of the size of one vibration per second is in this register (the great octave) not as disturbing as the difference between the natural and the Pythagorean thirds (80:81), but it is nevertheless large enough to be perceived by the ear. Yet it is the smallest possible difference, and it is in any case more acceptable than the one which would have arisen from the adoption of the G♭ (92.16) derived from the E♭.

The family has no further development. True, the D♭ could still produce an F♭ or a B♭♭, but we have better forms of these tones (E and A) already present; they would destroy the purity of our scale, and besides, we have already rejected F♭ in the course of our calculations. All the other great-grandchildren are already represented in our scale, and we need expect no further enrichment from the offspring of the great-grandchildren. Since the grandchildren already suffer from the disability of the comma, their descendants would veer off still further in the direction of the impure, and lose their harmonic connection with the original tone.

Moreover, our scale is complete: we need no further tones. If we arrange in ascending order from C to c all the tones we have derived, we shall find that the distances between the adjacent tones are not exactly the same throughout. They are in the proportions that occur in the third and fourth octaves of the overtone series: that is, 15:16, 16:17, 17:18, and 18:19. (For practical purposes the fractional parts of the vibration numbers may be disregarded.) All these intervals are heard as half-steps. The ear is not in danger either of mistaking the largest of these intervals (15:16) for a whole-step or of finding the smallest (18:19) too striking a departure from the normal half-step, such as would have resulted from the use of the abovementioned $-B\flat$ (112), $+B\flat$ (115.2), $-G\flat$ (89.6), $+G\flat$ (92.16) or $-E\flat$ (74.66). It follows from the inequality of the half-tones that the whole-tones too are of different dimensions; but they stay approximately within the limits set by 8:9 and 9:10.

Does not this inequality of interval-dimensions conflict with the requirement mentioned earlier of simple and clear relations, and of the maintenance of the half-step interval first produced—that between E and F? No, for in the first place the discrepancy is never so large as to result in loss of the relation to the model half-tone, and in the second place it is just the inequality in the distances between the tones that permits us to feel clearly the relations of the scale-tones to their progenitor. Thus in the scale derived from C the tone-succession c-d$\flat$-e$\flat$ would consist of an interval of 16:17 followed by an interval of 8:9; while in the scale derived from D$\flat$ the same succession would consist of 15:16 followed by 8:9, since in that scale the tones c-d$\flat$-e$\flat$ would occupy the positions that are held in the C scale by the tones b-c-d.

Guided by their subconscious feeling for the intervals, singers and players of string and wind instruments differentiate quite sharply between large and small whole-steps and half-steps. So long as they stay within the scale derived from a single fundamental generating tone (remember that the inclusion of the "children" and "grandchildren" does not imply any modulation), they produce the half-step and whole-step intervals according to our model series. When the generating tone changes, the tiny differences in the intervals change with it.

In equal temperament, there is no such adaptation to the fundamental tone, and thus to sensitive ears music performed on keyboard instruments lacks the fine lustre of the light that falls at ever-changing angles as it is cast by different generators. It does not have any of that fine inner agitation that arises from slight variations of pitch. That is why keyboard music may often grow somewhat tiresome if the player does not know how to make up for this natural shortcoming through such subtleties of performance as registration, dynamics, and touch.

[43]

11

The Comma

The last-cited example (c-d♭-e♭ = b-c-d) shows what happens to the comma in melodic and harmonic progressions. Players of keyboard instruments do not have to worry about it; it is divided up and so distributed on their instruments that the octave is pure and no other interval bears the entire burden of the comma. All other musicians—singers, and players of wind and string instruments—use untempered tuning. Guided by the ear, they dispose of the comma by always seeking to produce harmonic intervals in their simplest form. This means that they make all fourths and fifths pure, while the thirds and sixths vary slightly according to the melodic and harmonic functions of their constituent tones, and the remaining intervals are determined to suit the requirements of the invariable ones. The comma is thus relegated to intervals in which the ear will tolerate a certain impurity. This is not always accomplished without difficulty. It is often not possible, at the required speed of harmonic change, to produce the chords in their purest forms. In such instances, the harmonic intervals at the more important points are made pure, and the others brought as close to pure intonation as possible. If the harmonic and melodic progressions are such that the ear has difficulty in relating the fundamental tones to the scale-tones derived from them, while the chord structure consists only of simple triad formations, then this more or less even spreading out of the comma may be replaced by a more disjunct treatment: every chord appears in pure form, and the comma occurs, either in whole or in part, between it and its surroundings.

Singers and players achieve the solution of the comma problem for the most part without realizing it. Even in harmonic progressions which because of their complexity or quick succession can be comprehended only slowly, their ear leads them to relegate the comma to the least conspicuous place. When, however, the harmonic relations become too opaque, or when the roots of combinations follow one another in an order which is not unambiguous, the ear becomes uncertain. The singer or the player does not then know where to make the adjustment, and he sings or plays out of tune.

That is why passages based upon extreme chromaticism or enharmonic change are difficult—and for choral singers often impossible—to produce in pure intonation, even after all the experience that singers have had in the course of music history.

From this fact it is clear that musical practice, composition, and theory can never disregard the conditions laid down by the facts of the existence of pure intervals and the desire of the ear to perceive them wherever possible in tonal combinations. This does not mean that we must return to a more primitive level of harmonic and melodic practice. The harmonic and melodic material is, thanks to the constantly changing significance the composer can give it, infinitely variable. But all tonal phenomena are based upon inescapable facts, as they have been since men first began to make music, and will always be as long as they continue to do so. And these facts cannot be overlooked if order and purpose are to reign in music. Though the ear and the mind are capable of immense development in their ability to accept sounds of varying complexity, yet this ability depends on underlying natural phenomena, even though the latter usually lie hidden. Is it not superficial to try to attack phenomena so deeply rooted in the life of the soul as are the unconscious desire for the adjustment of the comma discrepancy, and the feeling for tonal relations in general, from so crassly physical a standpoint? We do not experience the relationships of tonal groups to the progenitor tones as a mathematical balance of vibration-numbers and ratios. It is not the derivation of scale-tones from the overtone series that causes our pleasure in listening to good music. What goes on in the realm of our emotions and sensations cannot be physically measured; indeed our procedure does not do justice even to the mere physical activity of hearing. Granted that, compared with the subtle spiritual stirrings which are the subject and object of our music-making, the observation of the overtone series with its quantitative relations is a rough and boorish procedure. Science knows much more refined methods of analyzing sound and hearing. But the crude facts of acoustics have one advantage: they are easy to observe and closely related to the instrumental handicraft that is in daily use by the musician. For him that which strikes the listener as an inner experience is first of all a matter of tuning the vocal chords, of lip-pressure, or of finger-placement. The most moving beauties of Mozart are for him in the first place notes on a page; the intervals, no matter what their effects on the soul, are tangible, measurable units; chords are light or heavy; tones have mass and density, just as solid objects do. He must, it is true, know more than anyone else about the beauty of his music, and must not be stupidly ignorant of what wise reflection upon its nature can reveal. But what good is the greatest wisdom to him if he does not know how to tune the vocal chords, to apply his lips, or to place his fingers in such a way as to produce the tonal structure that will move the listener?

For the composer, and consequently for everyone who concerns himself with the technique of composition, the same is true as for the good performer: he must achieve the deepest impression by employing the best possible devices. He will come by them much better through our materialistic approach than through many a learned discussion of the bases of musical procedure. Acoustic phenomena as a mirror of the life of the spirit have always represented the best point of departure for studies in the technique of composition, and we may assume that in the near future no better approach will be found, in spite of all the fruits of modern research. Perhaps some day a highly gifted thinker, equally accomplished in the fields of scholarly research and of music, will evolve new principles upon which to base a system of expounding the craft of musical composition—a system far clearer and more comprehensive than we can imagine. Until then it seems to me the more important to limit ourselves to the crude, easily understood basic facts, since in all branches of musical activity, nowadays, attention to simplicity of means and directness of effect is urgently needed.

12

Perspective

We have now listened carefully to the pure sound of the overtone series, we have examined the nature and tendency of the overtones, and we have thus found the simplest and most logical method of arranging the constituent parts of the overtone series (a vertically constructed series of which the parts are arranged one above another in proportional relations, forming unambiguous and immutable intervals) in a different series: the twelve-tone chromatic scale. This series, by means of tones ascending stepwise, reaches from a fundamental tone to the octave of that tone. The distances between the adjacent tones are all equal, except for tiny differences which do not affect our impression of equal distance, but rather permit us to infer the functions of each tone in relation to the fundamental tone of the series. The method we have used for determining the pitch of the tones of our scale is not replaceable by any of the methods commonly used for that purpose. The logarithmic method, or that which employs "cents", or any other division of the smallest pitch intervals, has no value for us, since none of these reveals anything about the most important aspect of our scale: the relation of the individual tones of the scale to their progenitor.

But I hear the reader who has attentively followed me thus far impatiently exclaim: "But what's the good of all this? The chromatic scale is nothing new. It would have been simpler to take it for granted as something generally known, and to have spared us all this reckoning, which is no pleasure for a musician!" To this I must reply that although the chromatic scale is known, it is so only as an enrichment or a variation of the seven-tone major and minor scales. All earlier theories of composition start from the seven-tone scale as the basis of musical creation, and in this they express a view generally held. My experience has taught me that to put forward any other opinion is to encounter unyielding opposition from both musicians and laymen. The situation today is like that which obtained at the time of the transition from the church modes to the major and minor scales, in the Middle Ages. Practice has gone forward to a point to which theory has not yet followed it. All composers nowadays make use of the extended harmonic and melodic relations that result from the use of the material of the chromatic scale, but for lack of an adequate theoretical foundation they still try to cram every manifestation within the narrow confines of diatonic interpretation.

[47]

Anyone who has once realized how many complicated and unclear explanations can be avoided by the assumption of the chromatic scale as the basic scale of musical theory, will feel like the man who has never deigned to pay any attention to the fire-escape outside his window until one day a fire breaks out, the stairs are in flames, and the scorned fire-escape becomes his only way out. From now on he will appreciate it. In music we have had a fire, too, and we are thankful not to have overlooked the escape provided by the chromatic scale.

The adoption of the chromatic scale as the basis of music does not mean that harmony and melody must consist of an uninterrupted series of whining half-tone slides, or that according to some arbitrarily conceived plan the tones of this scale must be scattered broadcast through our music, reappearing aimlessly in a thousand different forms. Everything that can be expressed in the diatonic system can be equally well expressed with this chromatic material, since the diatonic scales are contained in the chromatic. The advantages of tonal connection and of chordal and melodic interrelation are as much ours as they ever were. But we have thrown off chains that hampered our movement; we have discarded the tinted lenses that transformed the many-colored world around us into a dull and monotonous image.

In opposition to this view, the natural simplicity of the diatonic scales may be adduced. But the calculations which we have made demonstrate that the chromatic scale can be derived just as simply from the overtone series; that, since it makes exhaustive use of the clearest overtone relations, it has an even more natural basis; and that it is thus the most natural of all scales, and the best adapted to melodic as well as to harmonic use.

True, the pentatonic scale is a natural one. It is confined to the natural intervals of the octave, the fifth, and the fourth, and does not even make use of the major third to fill out its gaps. For us this represents the absence of the most important element of harmonic construction—the complete absence of the element of perspective. Just as the pentatonic scale permits only a monotonous and inflexible harmony (which is not stylistically suited to it, by the

Derivation of the Tones from C
(Chromatic Scale)

The tones through which the scale-tones are derived are enclosed in boxes. The series at the bottom gives the frequencies of the corresponding tones in equal temperament.

way), so the melodies that are based upon it are cool, undifferentiated, and remote. Thus even more for pentatonic than for other music we need to have a knowledge of the people who created it and their environment. Pentatonic scales still play an important rôle in Asia, but in European music they have been little used, because of the small number of tones they offer within the octave. Only slight relics of Irish and Scotch folk-music, with isolated fragments from other sections, testify to their former existence in Europe.

The old Greek scales, which in slightly changed form represented the modal material of mediaeval composition, certainly form noble bases for melodic construction. But they sprang so entirely from a melodic way of feeling, and were evolved so exclusively for melodic purposes, that they are like tracks that guide musical thinking into definite linear directions, although even the most strongly melodic means of expression always make use of certain harmonic elements. The church modes really began to die from the moment that the harmonic sense first sought expression in the earliest polyphony. Every simultaneous combination of tones really contradicts the nature of these scales, and can be explained in them only by patchwork additions to the modal system. The beginning of polyphony marks the beginning of the mastery of the diatonic major and minor scales. Yet for centuries men tried to explain the developing art of polyphonic writing in terms of scales not made for that purpose.

But surely major and minor scales form a rich body of material? It was they that first made the great development of our music possible, especially on the harmonic side. True; but did they not also favor the development of formulae and stereotyped turns of phrase which threatened to smother music? There have always been rebels against the tyranny of the major and minor—a few Italians at the end of the Renaissance (such as Gesualdo, Prince of Venosa) and above all Mozart, who in a number of his works shook the foundations of the major-minor régime.

The actual dethronement took place in the last century. In Wagner's *Tristan* the rule of major and minor was overthrown. Unquestionably, the diatonic scale was here replaced by the chromatic as the basis for all lines and harmonic combinations. But the revolu tion came too soon. The decision and the consistency of this bold step were unique, and at first no one followed the new trail. For decades *Tristan* remained the only work based on chromaticism, and even its creator never again made so mighty a forward step into the new domain. Not until the turn of the century did the outlines of the new world discovered in *Tristan* begin to take shape. Music reacted to it as a human body to an injected serum, which it at first strives to exclude as a poison, and only afterwards learns to accept as necessary and even wholesome. What we have experienced, instead of a true understanding of the chromatic world of music, has been first the penetration of an ever minuter chromaticism into the linear and harmonic aspects of our music, then the disintegration of every element, a lapse into complete absence of plan and rule, and finally pure anarchy.

If today, from our point of vantage over the whole field, we definitely adopt the chromatic scale as the basic material for composition, we are only continuing what was begun eighty years ago.

13

A Forward Glance

Will the musician forever be satisfied with this tonal material? Will there not be within some reasonable time a further enlargement of it? To many, the introduction of the quarter-tone system is the answer to this question.

Scales may arise, as we have seen, in either of two ways: through the filling out of the octave with intervals measured by the proportions of the overtone series, and through the arithmetical division of the octave. This book recommends the first of these, and the only way in which this system of scale-construction could be expanded would be by the use of the seventh overtone, for there is no compelling reason why we should choose arbitrarily among the proportions offered us by the overtone series, or skip over one of the overtones and choose the next one as a basis for further reckoning. But I have shown that to reckon with overtones above the sixth leads to chaos. The system cannot be enlarged in this direction.

The twelve-tone chromatic scale is, as far as we can humanly tell, the most complete solution of the problem—at least for harmonic purposes.

The quarter-tone system proceeds from the second method of scale-construction. It takes the equally tempered twelve-tone system as its point of departure. That is a mistake. We have seen that equal temperament does not offer a single scale-interval in pure form. But what can be borne in a twelve-tone system becomes intolerable in a system in which there are twice as many tones that contradict nature. Anyone who has heard quarter-tone music frequently, especially on keyboard instruments, knows that this is true, if his sense of hearing is healthy, and he has not allowed it to be clouded by preconceived opinions. Stringed instruments can make this music barely tolerable, since even when working with these intervals they can so place the comma that the ear hears pure intervals instead of an uninterrupted series of mistuned ones. But this must contradict the intention of the quarter-tone composer, for the correction of one of his intervals by the size of a comma is, proportionately, a considerable "clouding" of the interval. The assertion often made in support of the quarter-tone system—that quarter-tones exist in the folk-music of many peoples—is not true. All singers with a natural feeling for music employ not only the octave but also the pure fifth and pure fourth (which do not exist in the quarter-tone system). These intervals are then divided up into smaller ones, according to taste and tradition. The results include third-tones, fifth-tones, sixth-tones and of course also quarter-tones. But nothing indicates that any one of these small divisions is particularly favored. And how would it be possible to ascertain whether it were or not, since the untrained folk-singer will hardly reproduce with accuracy the same minute divisions each time he sings his song? To establish anything of this sort, it would be necessary to compare very exact measurements based on numerous phonographic recordings of the *same* singer singing the *same* song repeatedly.

For that matter, our own melody employs and always has employed intervals even smaller than the quarter-tone. A semitone for example, may, like any interval except the octave, fifth, and fourth, have infinitely varying dimensions, from the hardly perceptible departure from an original tone to the very close approximation of a whole-tone, depending on its melodic function. And of this great variety, based as it is on the highest sensitivity, the quarter-tone system would rob us for the sake of a decomposed harmony which, no matter how long we try to accustom ourselves to it, would no more satisfy our ears and spirit than concentrated food pills instead of a diet of naturally grown foods would satisfy the palate and the stomach.

Other expansions of the scale derived from the equally tempered system are, for the same reasons, necessarily sterile, whether based upon sixth-tones, eighth-tones, or any other divisions. So-called "pure intonation" instruments, in which a compromise is sought between the two types of scale-construction, are bound to have so many keys that they will always be too unwieldy to be of any use in musical practice.

Finally let us mention an aberration that has haunted and still haunts many inquirers: the micro-octave. It has been asserted that within the interval of a tone.or a semitone very detailed divisions could be made, which would exhibit relationships like those of the octave, the fifth, the fourth, and so on. It is true that the ear can perceive such tiny tonal divisions, as is shown by melodic performance, which makes use of such minute variations as a means of expression. But the theory does not hold. The simplest way to disprove it is simply to listen to such subdivisions. This is no longer impractical, for they can be produced electrically, and it will at once be apparent that there is no trace of any such structure as we know between a tone and its octave. Where, indeed, should such a structure come from? The structure of the true octave is derived from the overtone series, from which nothing more complete than the comprehensive building material furnished by the chromatic twelve-tone scale can be developed.

CHAPTER III

The Nature of the Building Stones

1

Series 1

A single tone conceived as the root of a scale; the chromatically arranged twelve-tone series born of the tensions set up by the juxtaposition of vibrating units in the proportions of the simple numbers from 1 to 6;—does not all this seem like a distant echo of the *musica mundana* of the ancients, of those harmonies of the spheres that reigned above both earthly types of music, *musica humana* and the music *"quae in quibusdam constituta est instrumentis"*? Those harmonies so perfect that the inadequate sense organs of men could not perceive them, needing no realization in sound, since the ratios of numbers that underlie all movement and all sound are more to the reflecting spirit than the external part of music—sound—through which it becomes profaned and is brought within the sphere of man's perceptions? For us there is no longer, thanks to our understanding of their common physical basis, a fundamental difference between *musica humana* and *musica instrumentalis,* and even as concerns *musica humana* and *musica mundana* we may concentrate our attention today rather on those aspects which they have in common than on those in which they differ. We shall not do as the ancients did, and carry over earthly relations to happenings far out in space. Rather, we shall observe in the tiniest building unit of music the play of the same forces that rule the movements of the most distant nebulae. This world harmony, which in its reality is infinitely more stimulating and for the musician more significant than the sounding hemispheres of the ancients, exists not only for the seeking and calculating knower of the stars; for the naive believer, too, it is a fact as real as it is inconceivable. But just as today an astronomer cannot understand his reckonings in light-years, or the equalization of time and space, without knowing the workings of the electrons within the cosmos of the atom, so to the believing musician the sense of his musical material, the earthly image of the harmonious music of the universe, can never be clear unless he continually returns to the deepest kernel of the single tone, and seeks to understand its electronic flux—the overtones in their proportional relations.

The nature of the atomic structure of music in the individual unrelated tone is already familiar to us, and we have followed the birth of the elements—the tones in the chromatic scale—from the electron-like relations of the overtones. And now we learn the *significance* of the tones. The order in which the tones of the scale were produced by the progenitor tone is of the greatest importance, in the view which this book represents. It is not only an indication that the tones have a family relationship, expressed in their connections to the principal tone; it is also an index to the *ranking* of these connections.

To a given tone, the tone an octave higher stands in so close a relationship that one can hardly maintain a distinction between the two. The tone which is only a fifth higher than the given tone is the next most closely related, and there follow in order the fourth, the major sixth, the major third, the minor third, and so on. As the distance from the given tone increases in this series, the relationship diminishes, until, in the tones that stand at the interval of the augmented fourth or diminished fifth, it can hardly be felt at all. This value-order of the relationships is valid under all circumstances. In every combination of tones, some tones must seem subordinate to others. The stronger ones may subject extended series of chords to their domination, or their rule may not last longer than a pulse-beat, but the accompanying tones will always be related to them according to the order laid down in our series. How benumbed our natural sensibilities must be nowadays, when systems of writing are put forward which are based on a complete lack of relationship among the tones. The carpenter would not think of disregarding the natural properties of his wood and putting it together any old way, without regard to its grain. The justification of such attempts to "expand" the musical language will be sought in vain in the tonal material itself. The only excuse for them must be the complaisant ear, which, despite the delicacy of its construction, is robust enough to accept sounds put together without the guidance of taste or instinct, instead of rejecting such sounds with the same unerring discrimination with which the senses of sight and touch would reject a chair thus miserably pieced together. In the domain of tonal relations no expansion or innovation is possible, no questions of style are applicable, and there can be no progress, any more than there can be in the multiplication table or the simplest laws of mechanics.

No other system gives us complete proof of the natural basis of tonal relations. All theorists are agreed, it is true, that there are various degrees of relationship, and the order of descending degrees of relationship is the same in all theories. This is remarkable, for in every other respect there is anything but unanimity among musical theorists. It seems as if a true feeling for the relationships had existed even without the only complete explanation of them, here given for the first time. To be sure, theorists have always sought to find those properties of the tonal material which might provide the logical basis for this feeling, and it cannot be denied that at least for the earliest relationships explanations have been found that are just as logical as ours. If, for example, one follows the overtone series up from any given fundamental, the closest relationships will be found between tones 1 and 2, 2 and 3, and 3 and 4, in the familiar order. But if one follows this series further, one will find a series of relationships wholly at odds with the experience of musical practice: tones related to the fundamental tone as 4:5 (major third), 5:6 (minor third), 6:7 (under-size third), 7:8 (over-size whole-tone), and 8:9 (large whole-tone) would be the

[55]

next most closely related tones after the fourth. To explain the tone that is really the next most closely related, the major sixth, it would be necessary to interrupt the process of following the over-tone series directly upwards (since the major sixth lies between tones 3 and 5); and for the derivation of the remaining tones from a single overtone series, in anything like the order that corresponds to practical musical experience, no rule can be found. This deriva-tion can only be arrived at arbitrarily, and thus would not furnish any theoretical justification for the experience of practice. The establishment of the major sixth as the interval 3:5 tells us the size of this interval, but not the degree of relationship of a tone which is a sixth above a fundamental tone.

We shall henceforth call the significant order in which the twelve tones of the chromatic scale made their appearance, in diminishing degree of relationship to the given tone, *Series 1*. The values of the relationships established in that series will be the basis for our understanding of the connection of tones and chords, the ordering of harmonic progressions, and accordingly the tonal progress of compositions. Just as in architecture the big supporting and con-necting members—piers, columns, girders, and arches—determine the form and size of a building, as well as its interior division into rooms, corridors, and floors, irrespective of the material of which they are built—so tonal relations introduce order into the tonal mass. Rhythm determines only its temporal succession. In our analogy, rhythm would determine the dimensions of the parts of the building and their distance from one another. Of course one cannot separate one function from the other. The supporting and connecting function of the columns cannot be separated from their place in space, and tonal relations must have definite rhythmic dimensions for their effect. But separate forces are nevertheless at work, as we see in places where one is much stronger than the other: where rhythm retreats far into the background in favor of a broad harmonic flow; or, on the other hand, where rhythm is the predominant element, and harmony and melody are hardly more than the coloring of the beats. How the tonal relations operate, we shall learn in Chapter IV.

Combination Tones

Up to now we have treated the tones only as members of a family, grouped about a progenitor tone. But a single tone is not music; unrelated and motionless, it cannot be called anything more than an "acoustic phenomenon". Even tonal relations, which form the basic principle for the organization of tonal combinations, are not in themselves music. The individual tone is not music until it is directly connected with other tones, and tonal relations are not operative until tones and tonal combinations are in motion. The primary building material of music must therefore include a third element, in addition to the tone and the principle of tone-relations. Music arises from the combined effect of at least two tones. The motion from one tone to another, the bridging of a gap in space, produces melodic tension, while the simultaneous juxtaposition of two tones produces harmony. Thus the *Interval,* formed by the connection of two tones, is the basic unit of musical construction. If we think of the series of tones grouped around the parent tone C (as in Series 1) as a planetary system, then C is the sun, surrounded by its descendant tones as the sun is surrounded by its planets. Series 1 shows us the distance of the planets from the central star. As the distance increases, the warmth, light, and power of the sun diminish, and the tones lose their closeness of relationship. The intervals correspond to the distances of the various planets from each other. In their *melodic* function, the two successive tones of an interval are like two planets at different points in their orbits, while the formation of a chord is like a geometric figure formed by connecting various planets at a given instant.

Just as the tone-relations are arranged in descending order of value, so the intervals have a natural order, which we shall call *Series 2.* Since we possess no material other than the twelve tones of the chromatic scale, they must also present the tonal material for Series 2. But here their significance is entirely different from what it was in Series 1, since we shall use Series 2 to evaluate the distances between the various tones, and not the relationship of each tone to the progenitor. The basic difference between the two series will be clear to us if we again think of the architectural function of their components in musical construction. Series 1 provided us with the principal members of the structure; Series 2 will furnish the smaller materials: bricks and mortar, rafters, floor-boards, lath and plaster. The stone that can only be made into a wall with thousands of other stones; the shingle that needs hundreds of other shingles and cross-pieces before the roof is complete—these things are not governed by the same rules as piers and girders. Even if the larger members are made out of the smaller ones, the properties of each of the latter are of importance only until the next similar unit is reached; the characteristics of these small building materials have little effect on the larger lines of the design. But it is only the knowledge of the properties of the smaller units that enables the builder to make walls, floors, and roofs out of them. We derived Series 1 from the overtone series. For Series 2 we must proceed to the examination of another natural phenomenon: combination tones.

When a stringed instrument plays a double stop, or two bassoons play together, or simultaneous groups of tones are produced in any other way, additional tones are involuntarily produced which bear the name of combination tones. They are usually so weak that the superficial ear does not perceive them, but this makes them all the more important for the subconscious ear. They are the third point of a triangle whose other two points are in the sounding interval, making possible for the ear a sort of trigonometry by which it is enabled to form a judgement of the purity of an interval. The musician who is not familiar with these phenomena had better impress clearly upon his mind the difference between overtones and combination tones. Overtones are produced in varying number by a *single* sounding tone; combination tones arise only when *two or more* tones sound simultaneously. How little the two phenomena have in common is shown by the simultaneous sounding of pure tones, having no overtones, previously mentioned as produced by special electrical means, or by tones poor in overtones, such as those produced by tuning forks. Such tones, poor or lacking in overtones, nevertheless produce combination tones; as a matter of fact, they produce them particularly easily.

Although the nature of combination tones has been known for a long time, they have never been applied in musical theory, in a degree appropriate to their significance, to the explanation of the properties of musical materials and the rules for musical writing. This is owing to the great pains formerly necessary to observe them and the meagre results obtained. Tuning forks and resonators, the classic tools for the investigation of combination tones, are inaccurate and clumsy weapons, to which they offer stubborn resistance. Today we have better tools, and while the appropriate experiments are not easily available to every musician, description of my own observations will enable him to follow my reasoning.

Many tone-colors are particularly favorable to the production of prominent combination tones. The latter can be clearly heard when two large tuning forks sound simultaneously, and the violinist hears them as soft bass tones when he plays double stops in pure intonation. Once the ear has become aware of them, it hears them easily, and in certain cases it hears the combination tones as strongly or even more strongly than the directly produced tones. This fact is of importance in instrument construction, as we see from a well known device among organ builders: in order to save the great expense and large amount of space required for the deepest labial pipes, builders of small organs who wish to provide for these very low tones take two smaller (higher) pipes which, when sounded together, will produce a combination tone of the desired pitch. From this fact we draw the important conclusion that an interval and its combination tone bear a certain immutable relation to each other, a conclusion confirmed by the following experiment.

Electric instruments for the production of tones permit us to let a given tone (say, c^1) sound uninterruptedly, with constant volume and timbre. In the following drawing, this sound is represented by the horizontal line starting at the point c^1.

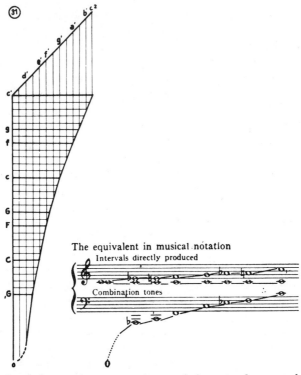

The equivalent in musical notation
Intervals directly produced
Combination tones

We then take another tone and move it in a steady upward glide, starting at the unison, c¹, and rising to c² (the oblique line c¹-c²). We can then hear, aided by sufficient amplification, a series of combination tones, also rising, which starts from zero (when the two tones are in unison), comes into being at a pitch so low as to be barely perceptible the moment we diverge ever so slightly from the unison, and forms, against the gradual ascent of the upper voice, a steeply rising curve. Towards the end of this curve the angle of the ascent decreases, and when the two main voices are at the interval of the octave the curve arrives at the pitch of the lower tone of that octave. The graphic representation of this procedure shows that beneath the played fifth we hear the octave below its lower tone, and beneath the fourth the double octave below its upper tone. That is, the simultaneous sounding of the tones c^1 (256 vibrations per second) and g^1 (384) produces the combination tone c (128), while the simultaneous sounding of c^1 (256) and f^1 (341.33) produces F (85.33). In other words, the fifth, corresponding to the overtones 4 and 6, carries with it a combination tone equal to overtone 2. Or, in ratios: the fifth 2:3 produces the combination tone 1; the fourth 3:4 (for the sake of comparison, we transpose the fourth c^1-f^1 of Figure 31 to g-c^1, the fourth in our original overtone series) likewise tone 1. From these facts we may deduce the principle governing the relation of the combination tone to the directly produced interval:

The frequency of the combination tone is always equal to the difference between the frequencies of the directly produced tones of the interval.

This principle also takes care of the ratios.

Interval directly produced									
Order numbers of the Overtone Series	2	3	4	5	4	5	6	8	8	10
	1	2	3	4	2	3	4	3	5	4
Differences	1	1	1	1	2	2	2	5	3	6
Vibration-frequencies	128	192	256	320	256	320	384	512	512	640
	64	128	192	256	128	192	256	192	320	256
Differences	64	64	64	64	128	128	128	320	192	384
Combination tones									

Combination tones, being real sounds, obey the same laws as other tones. As component parts of sounding intervals, they produce further combination tones, which are, of course, less intense than the first ones. If a combination tone consists of the difference between the proportion numbers (or frequency numbers) of two tones, then by the same process we have already used we can

[61]

easily find the combination tones of the second order. Let us take for example the minor third e¹-g¹ (320–384), which has the ratio 5:6. The first combination tone is the note 1, C, with 64 vibrations. This tone, in connection with one of the directly produced tones, results in a combination tone of the second order. The g¹ cannot be the tone that produces this second combination tone (in connection with the first), because it would produce nothing more than a change in intensity in the original interval: interval C-g¹ (1:6), combination tone e¹ (5). So it must be the interval C-e¹ (1:5) that produces the new combination tone—c¹ (4). If we find in this way the differences between the combination tones of the first order and the lower tones of the directly produced intervals, we shall arrive at the curve of combination tones of the second order.

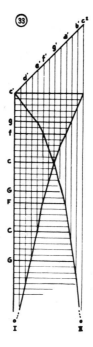

The equivalent in musical notation

Intervals directly produced

Combination tones:
○ 1st Order
◆ 2d Order

This curve goes in the opposite direction to the first: it begins at the unison with the directly produced tone, and sinks slowly, arriving beneath the played interval c'-e' at g, beneath c'-f' at f. Beneath the played fifth it intersects the first curve, and then sinks more quickly to zero, whence its opposite arose.

The series of combination tones of the second order combines with the intervals already present, consisting both of directly produced and of combination tones, to create new orders of combination tones. Theoretically, the system may be extended to infinity.

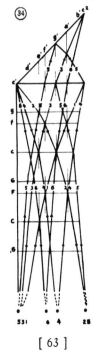

[63]

But we remember that the overtone series, too, is theoretically infinite. In practice it is hardly possible to produce audible combination tones of orders higher than the sixth. For the ear's sense of intervals the later orders of combination tones are without significance, since they are hardly perceptible even to the fine discriminations of the inner ear (of which we are not conscious), and since furthermore so long as the directly produced intervals are kept close to the simpler ratios of the overtone series, nothing is produced but octave doublings of earlier orders of combination tones. For the purposes of our discussion we shall therefore content ourselves with considering the combination tones of the first and second orders.

3

Inversions

We cannot hear combination tones produced by either the unison or the octave. For the unison, the first order of combination tones is at the zero point, and the second order coincides with the unison of the directly produced tones. For the octave, the second order is at the zero point, and the first coincides with the lower of the original tones. Combination tones represent a clouding or a burdening of the interval. The octave and the unison, as the most perfect intervals, are not subject to any such impurity; the fifth has only one combination tone, since those of the first and second order coincide; all other intervals carry a double burden of varying weight. The clouding of the intervals is not so strong that any effort need be made to suppress the combination tones. Yet of course they must not be so strong as to overshadow the directly produced interval. Provided they remain below the level at which they would become actually disturbing, they give the interval its characteristic stamp. An interval without combination tones would be an abstract concept, as bodiless as the ratio with which we express it numerically. Now, for the musician who, despite the intangibility of his building materials, is a healthy realist in his craft, numbers and intervals are of value only as sounding entities. He will accept cal-

[64]

culations employing proportions and curves only if they seem to offer practical advantages in the solution of musical problems. Thus the clouding of the intervals through the combination tones is not something that spoils his enjoyment of the abstract interval proportions; on the contrary, he uses it as a means of more precise perception of the intervals. The differences in the weight of the combination-tone burdens carried by the various intervals enables him to arrange the latter in order, so that starting with the octave, as the clearest, unclouded interval, and passing through the fifth (slightly clouded), each interval in succession carries a greater burden than its predecessors; that is to say, the purity and harmonic clarity of the intervals diminish step by step. In this series—Series 2 —we are accordingly setting up a list of the individual building stones according to strength, hardness, and density.

The fifth bears, as we have seen, but a slight burden:

Its two combination tones coincide at a point which doubles one of its tones at the lower octave. The fourth, too, shows a doubling of one of its factors:

But since these combination tones do not coincide, but are an octave apart, the fourth seems somewhat more heavily laden than the fifth.

The major third and the minor sixth, too, show doublings of one of their constituent tones in their combination tones. In the major

[65]

third the lower tone is doubled; in the minor sixth, the upper. Both have a new tone, in addition, not contained in the interval directly produced. The minor third and the major sixth, on the other hand, carry two such new tones. Thus we see that the intervals seem to pair off according to the arrangement of their combination tones. The two members of each pair have the same combination tones. The only difference is that the second interval of each pair seems to reverse the relations of the combination tones (in this connection we disregard octave transpositions). If in the first interval the combination tone of the first order forms the fundamental of the whole tonal composite, then in the second interval of the same pair this tone takes the place which the second-order tone had in the first interval: in this second interval, the second-order tone becomes the bass. The major third c^1-e^1 has combination tones in the positions C (first order) and g (second order); and the minor sixth e^1-c^2 has c (second order) and g (first order), as may be easily seen by transposing upward the minor sixth c^1-ab^1 in Fig. 37. The intervals thus pair off as follows: fifth and fourth, major third and minor sixth, minor third and major sixth, major second and minor seventh, minor second and major seventh.

Here we have a purely acoustical proof of the invertibility of intervals. That intervals are invertible, and that an interval adds up with its inversion to an octave, could hitherto be proved only from the ratios of the overtone series: the inversion of the major third 4:5 is the minor sixth 5:8 (5:2 × 4); the inversion of the minor third 5:6 is the major sixth 6:10 (or, in reduced terms, 3:5). Considering the above-mentioned dislike of most musicians for figures and other abstractions, proof offered by the combination tones ought to appeal to them more than that from the mere ratios, the more so as it provides us at the same time with another important item of knowledge: *the two intervals that make up each pair are of unequal value.* In order to understand that statement, let us keep two facts clearly in mind:

[66]

1. In groups of tones of different pitch sounding simultaneously, the deeper tones, with the slower vibration rates, have greater weight than the higher ones (a fact based on the weight of the vibrating material—the air masses).

2. Combination tones of the first order are significantly louder than those of the second order.

In the combination tones that arise from a major third, the lower, because of its low pitch, has the greater weight:

And it also (as a combination tone of the first order) surpasses its companion in intensity. The combination tones that belong to the inversion of the major third (minor sixth), on the other hand, present a less clear picture. Here too, of course, the lower tone (the doubling of the upper of the two directly produced tones) is the heavier; but it lacks the confirmation of this advantage which its prototype in the major third had. This tone is only the weaker combination tone of the second order, and is surpassed in intensity by the combination tone of the first order, which lies above it. It does not achieve the effect that is really due it, as the doubling of one of the original tones of the interval, because of the competition of its more intense but less significant companion (less significant in its relation to the tonal composite formed by the original interval and its combination tones). The aural impression created by the major third is thus distinctly clearer and more definite than that of the minor sixth. In the interval-pairs, both thirds and seconds show this more favorable disposition of their combination tones as compared with their inversions (sixths and sevenths). Between the fifth and the fourth the difference is not so marked, since the first-order combination tone lies below the second in both, whereas all other inversions exhibit the opposite disposition. But despite this favorable arrangement of the combination tones, the fourth is inferior to the fifth. The coincidence of the two combination tones of the fifth gives it a purity which makes it superior to all other intervals except the octave.

<h1 style="text-align:center">4</h1>

<h2 style="text-align:center">Interval Roots</h2>

We have learned two lessons from our consideration of the combination tones—the proof of the invertibility of intervals, and the determination of the relative value of the intervals. A third awaits us.

If one of the tones of the directly produced interval is doubled, either in the unison or in a lower octave, by a combination tone, this accretion of strength gives it the upper hand over its partner. In intervals in which such doublings occur, the constituent tones are thus not of equal value. Rather, the tone strengthened by such doublings is to be regarded as the *root* of the interval, and the other as its subordinate companion. Numerous experiments have convinced me that the feeling that one tone of an interval has more importance than the other is just as innate as the ability to judge intervals exactly—everyone hears the lower tone of a fifth as the principal tone; the ear cannot be persuaded to attribute primary importance to the upper tone. Yet I have never found in any treatise the statement that intervals have roots—a curious circumstance, since this fact is of primary significance for the hearing and evaluation of harmonic intervals, and since its acoustical basis is so easily established:

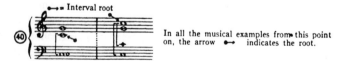

In all the musical examples from this point on, the arrow ●→ indicates the root.

The lower tone of the fifth is the root. The fact that both combination tones coincide at the lower octave of this tone makes it doubly strong; that is why the impression of the lower tone as root is so unmistakable, and the fifth is so very stable. In the fourth, the upper tone is doubled by the combination tones, and thus it is not

[68]

the heavier lower tone that has the effect of a root. The interval is thus less steady than the fifth.

In the next pair of intervals, too, the root of the more stable major third is at the bottom, and of the minor sixth at the top.

The new tone introduced by the combination tones converts this interval into a triad, of which the root is doubled. The triad is not present in full strength, to be sure; yet it is so clearly represented that the rules of harmony permit the use of the "triad without its fifth"—a contradiction of the definition of a triad as consisting of three tones, while this interval contains only two. This pair of intervals offers a particularly clear example of the inferiority of the second interval, the minor sixth, in harmonic value. The major third contains in the pleasantest disposition the doubling of its lower tone by the first-order combination tone, while the new tone, which completes the triad, lying a fourth below the lower tone of the original interval, is appropriately weaker, being a combination tone of the second order. In the minor sixth, on the other hand, the root, which, because in the directly produced interval it is higher than its companion tone, is to that extent already weaker, is doubled only by a combination tone of the second order. The latter does, to be sure, lie in the bass, but because of its weaker intensity it is less prominent than the less important first-order tone which completes the triad. Obviously so ambiguous a tonal structure must produce a less satisfying effect than that of the major third.

The next pair of intervals consists of the minor third and its inversion, the major sixth.

Neither of the original tones is represented among the combination tones; instead, a new tone occurs, doubled in the octave, which again converts the interval into a major triad, but this time a major triad of which the root is not one of the original tones. That is, beneath the minor third lies the lower fifth of its upper tone, and beneath the major sixth the lower fifth of its corresponding lower tone. The minor third has the better disposition of the combination tones, since its first-order tone lies in the bass, whereas the lowest tone of the composite formed by the major sixth and its combination tones is the less intense combination tone of the second order. Since the new tone, not represented in the original interval, occurs in two different octaves among the combination tones, and since, lying below the original tones, it possesses greater weight than they, it fulfills all the requirements of a root. This confronts us with the somewhat surprising necessity of placing under every minor third and major sixth a tone which is not represented either in the directly produced interval or, of course, in its notation. Here theory comes into conflict with the practice of composition, which likes to deal with things that are clearly to be heard and seen, and would therefore like to take one of the two tones of the directly produced interval as its root. Practice could perfectly well yield to the theoretical requirement without the slightest hindrance, as long as the minor third and the major sixth appeared alone—that is, in two-part writing only. But as soon as these intervals appear in combination with others, which is by far the most usual practice in our music, the observance of this theoretical requirement would make our analysis far too difficult and too different from our habitual point of view, so that it seems more advantageous to treat both intervals according to the pattern which we have derived from their predecessors in the series. This would make the lower tone of the minor third, and the upper tone of the major sixth, the root.

Another consideration, besides ease in treatment and analogy with the root-determination of the other intervals, speaks for this procedure. This is the fact that whenever minor thirds and major sixths appear as parts of richer tonal combinations, they are almost always subordinate to stronger and more important intervals, so that it is unnecessary to set up a separate rule to cover the few instances in which these intervals are of governing importance, merely to satisfy theoretical requirements. We do not deny the existence of the real roots of these intervals, or their significance, nor does the system here set up as a natural and logical basis for musical composition suffer any lacuna on this account. We are simply making use of a convenient labor-saving device to render these intervals easier to handle. Whoever rejects this aid, even though such aids have always been adopted in practice, and prefers to make his study of musical writing more complicated in order to stick absolutely close to theory, may take the real root established by the combination tones as the root of every minor third and major sixth he uses.

Our decision makes it possible for us to use both intervals without hesitation. But if, although we need seek no farther, we insist on looking for an acoustical justification for the step we have taken, we may examine a little more closely the thirds that exist in the lower part of the overtone series. (The basis thus arrived at, however, will not change anything connected with the combination-tone structure of the minor third and the major sixth as explained above, and will not furnish a complete proof.) Within the first 11 overtones alone there are five different sizes of thirds:

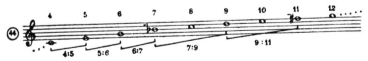

the major 4:5, the minor 5:6, the under-sized 6:7, the over-sized 7:9, and the one which is between major and minor, 9:11. To these we may add the Pythagorean third, which we can easily calculate (see page 30), and which is between 4:5 and 7:9 in size. The ear

[71]

not only hears all these as thirds; it permits itself to be hood-winked still further by this beautiful but characterless interval. If we play on the violin or other appropriate instrument a third that is as small as it can be without being a second, and if we then slide the upper tone up to the upper boundary of the third, just below the point where it would become a fourth, we cannot say just where the change from a minor third to a major third takes place.

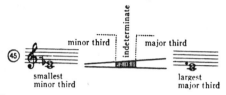

In the middle space between the outside boundaries there is a field that can belong to either third, and is assigned by the ear to the major or the minor according to the harmonic or melodic context. With an interval that is so indefinite we can well afford to allow ourselves the liberty proposed.

Those intervals whose tones are separated by such great distances that they seem to be octave transpositions of fifths, fourths, etc., present much less happy dispositions of the combination tones than their prototypes, and accordingly justify the usual view, confirmed by a long history in musical practice, which assigns to them lower harmonic values, diminishing as the distance between their constituent tones increases. Even the octave, which stands above and beyond all calculation of interval values, loses so much of its value when it appears in the form 1:4 that, as its combination-tone structure shows, it is hardly equal to the fifth in clarity. In the form 1:8 the harmonic support of the interval by its combination tones is still less strong, and in the form 1:16 the composite becomes completely dissonant. Although all these forms are exceptional, adapted only to particularly characteristic and striking effects, and consequently seldom concern us as building material for the craft of composition based on a normal harmonic foundation, they are not useless. True, they seldom occur except as parts of chords containing one, two, or even more additional constituents,

[72]

which take away the empty effect of the extended two-tone interval. But one might assume from the disposition of the combination tones of these intervals that when they did occur unmixed their effect would be much worse than it actually is. The fact that it is not is owing to the overtone series of the lower constituent tone of the interval, which is not disturbed by the comparatively strong combination tones that lie between the two tones of the interval, and which instead takes over their functions and fills in, sparsely but adequately, the large tonal expanse. When the tones of the interval are normally close together, the narrowness of the space and the force of the combination tones prevent any effect of the overtone series on the harmonic content of the interval.

The fifth in the position 1:3 still presents an excellent tonal picture; even 1:6 is good; not until 1:12 does it begin to lose value, although the freely unfolding overtone series of the lower tone of the fifth prevents it from becoming altogether worthless. The fourth is strikingly less fortunate—3:8 is still good, though a bit unstable; but 3:16 has no harmonic value (and who would think of introducing the fourth 3:16 into an otherwise smooth two-voiced texture?). That is owing not only to the combination tones, but also to the strong overtone series of the lower tone, in which the upper does not occur. The intervals after the fifth and the fourth lose their harmonic value in such octave transpositions even faster, and the inverted intervals (sixths) are, as one might expect, even worse off than the thirds.

[73]

The question then arises how these widely spread intervals are to be treated, for although in simple writing they never appear, and in the more complicated forms they occur only seldom, still we must know how to use them and what rank to ascribe to them. For this purpose one might determine separately the root of each of them, by experiment and by analogy, and then one would simply have to learn these roots by heart, in order to have them readily at hand when they were needed. But there is no point in going to all this trouble for a few exceptional cases. It is more practical here, too, to take a short cut, and to handle the spread intervals exactly like their close prototypes. This is quite sufficient for the practical purposes of composition.

5

The Minor Triad

In connection with the above description of the nature of the third we must mention a chord that has always given theorists endless trouble—the minor triad. To understand and explain the major triad is a task made easy for us by Nature, who places it in our hands as a handsome gift. But she gives us no hint about the minor triad. It does not occur in the overtone series, at least not in three successive tones. In the upper reaches of the series, minor triads ·can be constructed by skipping some tones (10:12:15); but this seems too far-fetched an explanation of a chord that appears almost as valuable as the easily explainable major triad.

We have seen that the value of a harmonic interval is determined by the grouping of its combination tones. The euphony of the major triad must accordingly be based not only on its favored position in the overtone series, but also on the disposition of its combination tones. In the major triad c^1-e^1-g^1

the major third c¹-e¹ produces the combination tone C (first order) and g (second order); the minor third e¹-g¹ produces C and c¹; and the fifth c¹-g¹ only c. The directly produced triad is strengthened in the most complete way by the combination tones. How unfavorable, in comparison, is the picture presented by the minor triad. In the triad c¹-e♭¹-g¹

the minor third c¹-e♭¹ produces the combination tones A♭₁ and a♭; the major third e♭¹-g¹ produces E♭ and b♭; and the fifth c¹-g¹ produces c, as in the major triad. All that the combination tones tell us about the minor triad is that it is of less harmonic value than the major.

Almost all explanations of the minor triad have proceeded from the assumption that it is based on the converse of the natural principle of tonal construction. According to them the minor triad is a mirror image of the major. Within the boundaries of the fifth, the thirds are said to be so arranged that the order "major third, minor third" of the major triad is reversed in the minor. That is not hard to see, but it does not prove anything. In working with an element tied to the principle of gravity as closely as tone is, one cannot simply turn things upside down for the sake of a pretty idea. Every tonal composite is constructed from the bottom up; that is determined by the nature of the tonal world. Tones obey the laws exemplified in the overtone series just as the stones piled one upon another to make a building obey the laws of statics that apply in nature.

The cleverest of all the explanations based on the thirds contained within the fifth in the two triads is the one that says that the origin of the minor triad is in man's desire to transfer to the world of tone the symmetry of his body. Since the major triad, on account of the inequality of its thirds, is an asymmetric structure, its opposite must be erected to restore the balance. This would be

[75]

convincing if other instances of such efforts to erect symmetrical counterparts were to be found in music. In the domain of *visual* forms, symmetry is one of the most important principles of design; tonal and temporal phenomena, on the other hand, seem to avoid it. Except in a few of the simplest basic rhythmic and formal elements (measure-rhythm and the simplest song-forms), it is hardly to be found in the field of *aural* forms. It is true that every more or less extended musical form consists of parts which offset each other to maintain the tonal balance of the whole. They are usually of unequal weight, since the juxtaposition of equal weights (a truly symmetrical arrangement) does not satisfy the listener. Hence the rule that when a section is repeated, or when a later section corresponds to an earlier one, changes of a formal nature—*i. e.,* abbreviations or expansions—must be made. The extremely few examples of strictly symmetrical structure in musical works of recognized worth (except where other features eclipse the formal design) are the exceptions that prove the rule. Against the theory of symmetrical construction is also the fact that while it is true that we have a minor triad that is the opposite of the major, we do not have any opposite of the complete major tonality, which may be represented by its major triads on the fourth, fifth, and first degrees, in the shape of a really independent minor tonality. In harmonic progressions we make no distinction between the major and minor modes. Only the triad on the first degree tells us which mode is meant; all the other triads exist in both modes with major and minor thirds. A major dominant is the rule in minor, and the minor subdominant is fully at home in major, as are the Neapolitan and other alterations. Indeed, one form of the minor scale, the upward melodic, is the same as the major with the single exception of the minor third, and the fact that the other forms differ more importantly is due to a desire to reconcile the sixth degree with its close relative, the third: it is felt to be undesirable that an augmented fourth should exist between these two degrees. Thus there is no sign of symmetry between the major and minor modes.

A more daring explanation is the one that assumes a different effect of the overtones in the major and minor triads. The three overtones 4:5:6 that make up the major triad (c^1-e^1-g^1 in the series based on C) have a common fundamental, of which the first tone of the triad forms the octave, while the second and third tones form the third and fifth.

The minor triad is said to exhibit the opposite relations. When it is in the corresponding close position, its three tones are said to have in the g^3 a common overtone, which bears the relation of fifth, third, and octave, to the root, third, and fifth of the triad respectively. It is not clear why in one case a lower tone (fundamental or combination tone) and in the other a higher tone (overtone) should be adduced. The basic error of this explanation is, however, that it reckons with actual tonal relations which are no sooner cited in the case of one triad than they are disregarded in the case of the other. If the overtones of the minor triad are significant, then so are those of the major triad. But then we should have between the two g^3s, which occur as the overtones of the c^1 and the g^1, a $g\sharp^3$, as the fifth overtone of the e^1:

And here the whole house of cards collapses, for the minor triad should rank higher in the scheme of tonal values than the major, since its overtones are better arranged.

The most far-fetched and at the same time the most interesting explanation of the minor triad is the one based on the undertone series. The latter is the exact inversion of the overtone series:

[77]

It seems to me repugnant to good sense to assume a force capable of producing such an inversion. This force would do away with the gravitation that is expressed in the overtone series—and there is no evidence of the operation of such a force. In electro-acoustics there is a familiar phenomenon that it would be easy to mistake for an undertone series. Electric tone-producers can be made to sound, in connection with a given tone, combination tones having a wave-length twice, three times, four times and so on (and accordingly having a frequency one-half, one-third, one-fourth and so on) that of the given tone. This remarkable phenomenon, caused by the intersection points of the electric waves (and consequently of the air-vibrations), can never have for music the same significance as the overtone series. It occurs only under certain conditions, which were not possible before the days of electric tone-production, and which can never be produced by vibrating strings, pipes, or membranes. This "undertone series" has no influence on the color of the tone, and lacks the other natural advantages of the overtone series which arise without any artificial help and are available anywhere and anytime. Thus we have here no proof of any inversion of the overtone series occurring freely in nature. This phenomenon, which actually exists for the ear, does offer, like the purely theoretical undertone series, a tempting picture of the minor triad outlined by its first six tones. And yet even with special apparatus or with the help of the Dualistic theory we learn nothing about the minor triad except that it is the opposite of the major. For that we do not need the undertone series; the simple principle of interval inversion suffices.

What, then, is the minor triad, in reality? I hold, following a theory which again is not entirely new, that it is a clouding of the major triad. Since one cannot even say definitely where the minor third leaves off and the major third begins, I do not believe in any polarity of the two chords. They are the high and low, the strong and weak, the light and dark, the bright and dull forms of the same sound. It is true that the overtone series contains both forms of the third (4:5 and 5:6) in pure form, but that does not alter the fact that the boundary between them is vague. Pure thirds furnish us with pure forms of both major and minor triads. But the ear allows within the triads, too, a certain latitude to the thirds, so that on one and the same root a number of major triads and a number of minor triads can be erected, no two alike in the exact size of their thirds. Triads in which the third lies in the indeterminate middle ground can, like the third itself, be interpreted as major or minor, according to the context. But why the almost negligible distance between the major and minor thirds should have such extraordinary psychological significance remains a mystery.

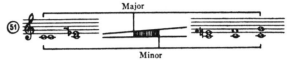

It seems as if this middle ground between the thirds were a dead point in the scale, to which another similar but less significant dead point corresponds—the middle ground between the two species of sixths. Up to this point the harmonic force of the tonic has been working up from the bottom; here begins the dominance of the fourth and fifth, which extends from the boundary between the thirds to that between the sixths. Thus the minor triad would be associated with rest, and would derive from this fact its heavy, dull character. The major triad, of which the third lies in another field of force, would then receive from the active, life-giving sources other than the tonic its impulse, light, and energy.

6

Seconds and Sevenths; The Tritone

For the practical application of the next two pairs of intervals— major second and minor seventh, minor second and major seventh —it makes no difference which of the tones we take as the root. The combination tones do not point to definite conclusions. Seconds and sevenths are subject to greater variation than any other intervals; in both melody and harmony they occur in the greatest variety of sizes. A glance at our table of combination tones shows us that even

[79]

slight changes in the sizes of intervals have important consequences for the disposition of the combination tones.

If we transpose all the seconds that occur in the overtone series between tones 7 and 11 so that they have a common lower tone, then the undersized major second c^1-d^1 (10:11)

has the combination tones Ab_2 and $+bb$;

the major second (minor whole-tone) c^1-d^1 (9:10)

has the combination tones Bb_2 and bb

the major second (major whole-tone) c^1-d^1 (8:9)

has the combination tones C_1 and $-bb$

the oversized major second c^1-d^1 (7:8)

has the combination tones D_1 and a.

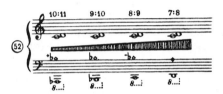

The situation is reversed, of course, for the minor seventh.

The minor second and major seventh exhibit still more complex dispositions of their combination tones. If we do not wish to make our work impossibly complicated, we must renounce hair-splitting distinctions between the various sizes of seconds and sevenths. We shall assume for each interval a normal size representing the average of the possibilities. The choice of a root is made more difficult by the wide choice of combination tones. It would be very tempting to take the lower tone of the second c^1-d^1 as the root, because of the combination tone C_1 produced by the major whole-tone. Practical considerations, however, lead me to choose the upper tone as the root. Our familiarity with the dominant seventh chord leads us to hear the *lower* tone of the seventh belonging to this composite as the root, even when it appears alone:

At least this choice seems more natural than the opposite one. As the inversion always has the root in the opposite position, the *upper* tone becomes the root of the major second. We treat the pair consisting of the minor second and major seventh in exactly the same way: the root of the second is at the top, and of the seventh at the bottom. The objections of the doubter who made himself heard earlier, when we chose the roots of the minor third and major sixth, will no doubt be more vehement this time. In self-defense I can again cite the practice of composers. And to dissipate all doubts I suggest that the attempt be made once to find the true acoustic roots of all the seconds and sevenths one works with, among the many possibilities. Anyone who once carries out this very laborious procedure will soon enough find justification for avoiding undue complication of his work. For he would have to spend ten times as much time and trouble on determining the exact size of the intervals as on writing them.

To complete Series 2 we still need one interval: the tritone. This is the name given since time immemorial to the augmented fourth, reflecting its construction of three superposed whole-tones. The term does not really fit the enharmonically equivalent diminished fifth. But because of our constant use of chromatic and enharmonic formations, we differentiate between the two intervals nowadays only on paper, so that I do not hesitate to group both intervals under the name tritone. The tritone does not make a pair with any other interval. It stands at the end of the series of pairs, as the counterpart to the octave that stands at the beginning:

The octave is the proudest, the noblest of the intervals, and does not mingle with the others; the tritone is the most distant relative, the eccentric, barred from close association with the interval pairs like Loki among the gods of Valhalla—and similarly indispensable.

The tritone has no root. It is accompanied by combination tones that stand in an unusual relation to it.

[81]

When its two tones are in their closest position (5:7), the combination tones form a fifth which combines with the tritone to make a seventh-chord, in which the lower tone of the tritone is the third, and its upper tone (although too low) the seventh. In the opposite, widest position (7:10) the combination tones form a fourth. The latter combines with the tritone to form a four-three chord, in which the lower tone of the tritone is the seventh, and the upper the third of the chord. All the tritone intervals that lie between these two extremes produce seventh chords which are between the two given above. Consequently, the tritone always has a dominant effect. It is characterized by a tendency towards a tonic, a tendency most naturally satisfied by a progression which takes the form of a "resolution" to the progenitor tone of its family (complemented by one or more tones which form with it either an interval or a chord). But already we see the dual nature of the tritone: if the preceding interval-successions have not made the relationship to a progenitor clear, one has the choice between two equally good resolutions. And in the resolution, the ear always hears one of the tones of the tritone as a leading tone to the root of the following tonic chord:

But since the ear cannot at once decide which of the tones of a tritone heard without clear family relations is the leading tone, it is always uncertain in its reaction to this interval. On the one hand the tonal uncertainty of the tritone, which makes it vaguer and more opalescent than any other interval, and on the other its strong urge for resolution, which at the moment of progression monopolizes the attention—this combination of indefiniteness and tension is what distinguishes the tritone, and makes it a foreign body and a ferment among the intervals.

[82]

Although this sanctimonious interval, at once obscure and in-
sistent, permits us neither from its aural effect nor from its acoustic
construction to declare one of its tones the root, we must at any
rate, in order to handle it at all, be able to decide from case to case
which of its tones is the more important. The sound of the interval
itself artfully conceals from us any answer to this question, and we
must draw our conclusions from its environment. From the tone,
chord, or interval to which the tritone resolves we see to which
family-progenitor it belongs. We shall consider that member of the
tritone which proceeds *by the smallest step* to this progenitor (the
root of the resolution interval) as the *root representative*.

In all examples from this point on,
the sign ▶—→ will indicate the
root representative.

We can easily understand how the tritone has in all periods of
music history held its unique position among the intervals. Instrumental music has arrived at a *modus vivendi* with it, aided more or
less by the mechanization of its method of determining the pitches
of the tones. But to the singer, especially the choral singer, it is
still loathsome. Musical theory has always been at odds with the
"diabolus in musica", and has always treated it with a peculiar
mixture of love and hatred. Theorists at first tried to get around it.
The Greeks avoided it by the interpolation of a complementary
tetrachord (*synemmenon*) among their four regular ones. In the
church modes the device used was the substitution of *B rotundum*
for *B quadratum*. The rules for organum and descant excluded
the tritone, and its revenge was that this exclusion prevented them
from prospering. Then a settlement was made: the treatises of
mediaeval theorists are an endless chain of attempts to accommodate the *"mi contra fa";* solmization is the attempt to take in
the unwelcome guest with impunity. Finally, the tritone became
the pet of harmony, through the outstanding importance given to
all chord formations serving as dominants, through the harmony of
Tristan and the chromaticism that followed in its wake, and even
through such flimsily based devices as the whole-tone system that

[83]

flourished about the turn of the last century. For us, who have now learned the position of the tritone within the family of intervals, and the grounds of its claim to that position, it has lost its terrors. Yet even for us it remains a civilized demon—*"der Geist, der stets verneint"*: the spirit that ever denies.

7

Significance of the Intervals

The inclusion of the tritone completes Series 2. To refute once and for all the superficial observation that might be made—to the effect that Series 1 and Series 2 are so much alike, except for a slight difference as concerns the thirds and sixths, that the setting up of two series is superfluous—let us once more state briefly the difference between them.

Series 1 consists of *tones*, in relation to a progenitor tone from which they derive their tonal position. Series 2 consists of *intervals*, without relation to a progenitor tone. (Instead of taking c^1 as the point of departure for our interval series, we could perfectly well have taken a different tone as the basis of each interval, without disturbing the orderly procedure of our investigation in the slightest; whereas in the construction of Series 1 that would not have been possible.) In the following example:

the effect of Series 1 is such that the g^1, as fifth of the c^1, assumes a preferred status. The a^1, as major sixth of c^1, is less closely related, and the e^1, as major third, even less closely. (As we shall see later, Series 1 will not be used for the analysis of such small tonal groups; it will be reserved for higher purposes, and is instanced here only for the sake of comparison.) Series 2, on the other hand, tells us that the *skip* of a fifth (g^1-c^1) is stronger in harmonic effect than the skip of a fourth (e^1-a^1), which latter, however, is stronger than the third c^1-e^1 or the second a^1-g^1.

The value-order laid down in Series 2 brings us close to the question of the consonance or dissonance of intervals. The interval-pairs do not indicate by a gap of any kind that there is any point at which the consonances stop and the dissonances begin. The two concepts have never been completely explained, and for a thousand years the definitions have varied. At first thirds were dissonant; later they became consonant. A distinction was made between perfect and imperfect consonances. The wide use of seventh-chords has made the major second and the minor seventh almost consonant to our ears. The situation of the fourth has never been thoroughly cleared up. Theorists, basing their reasoning on acoustical phenomena, have repeatedly come to conclusions wholly at variance with those of practical musicians.

Our investigation dissipates the fog that has hitherto prevailed. We know that no point can be determined at which "consonance" passes over into "dissonance". We can afford to let these terms stand for the extreme boundaries of the satisfying and unsatisfying effect of intervals and chords. The consonant intervals would then appear at the beginning of Series 2 and the dissonant at the end. But the rate at which the consonance of the intervals near the beginning decreases and the dissonance of those near the end increases cannot be determined exactly. Between the octave as the most perfect and the major seventh as the least perfect intervals, there is a series of interval-pairs which decrease in euphony in proportion as their distance from the octave and their proximity to the major seventh increases. The tritone belongs neither to the realm of euphony nor to that of cacophony; here again, as a unique interval, it remains outside our classification.

We have constructed Series 2 on the basis of the combination-tone curves, in the order of increasing complexity. The history of Western music has followed the same path through the centuries in its recognition of the values of the harmonic intervals. The ear at first recognized only single, monophonic lines, consisting of nothing but fundamental tones (tones numbered 1 in the overtone series). In the course of time, proceeding from interval to interval, it discovered the secret of composites consisting of two or more tones, the secret contained in the combination tones. Singing in octaves occurred before the earliest beginnings of polyphony, as the natural consequence of the participation of voices of different registers. Successions of parallel fifths and fourths were the first polyphonic devices; and gradually the value of thirds and sixths became apparent. The tritone was—here, too—an exception: it appeared comparatively early, as a component of independent harmonic formations. This would seem curious if we did not know that uninterrupted successions of triads seemed to the musical ear, even in the earliest polyphony, a too unalloyed pleasure. Composers met the ear's desire for a more intense sound by introducing the tritone in its mildest form: the first inversion of a diminished triad. The intervals between the pairs of tones contained in this chord are only, apart from the tritone, the minor third and the major sixth; the harsher seconds and sevenths are still lacking. They slipped into harmonic combinations late in the development, and then only by the side-entrance of melodic function (passing tones), until at the end of the seventeenth century the ear had learned to accept them, too, as independent intervals, usable for harmonic purposes. The tritone lies at the top of the inverted diminished triad; the important bass tone is free to move, unhampered by the tritone. Even today, minor seconds and major sevenths have not attained full equality with the other harmonic intervals; and a thousand years of familiarity will not achieve it for them.

For intervals are not like clay, which receives an impression and faithfully preserves it until the next one comes along and effaces it; they are elastic, rather, like steel, and although they vary in hardness, none of them is completely pliable. If we spoke earlier of breaking the will of the tones, this must have meant that we must see to it that the force that is latent in the intervals must be prevented from simply acting freely as it chooses—not that we could by main force stamp the raw material into any shape, without regard to its natural elasticity. Under wise treatment, the tonal material can be easily bent and welded. But if too great a strain is put upon it, or if it is not handled in accordance with the laws of its own nature, it will break like any other building material, and the music constructed from it will be useless.

8

Harmonic and Melodic Value of the Intervals

Every tonal movement arises from the combined working of harmonic and melodic forces—to ignore the rhythmic element for the moment. Harmony is the more robust of the two elements. It has its own tendencies and it is hard to force. There are many possible harmonic combinations, and the gradations between them are innumerable. The very quantity of the material commands the composer's thorough consideration, and "inspiration" and "invention" can be effective only on the basis of adequate technical knowledge. The novice will hardly succeed in traversing the harmonic territory, which abounds in a wealth of the most manifold phenomena. Melody is less aloof. Many a dilettante, who has no conception of the craft of the composer, gives birth to pleasant melodic ideas. The melodic material is easier to conquer, being of limited extent, and light and airy as compared with the harmonic. But it is also more deceptive. In no field are taste, musical culture, and genuine inclination or the lack of it more important than in melody.

Harmony and melody are complementary elements. Neither is strong enough to stand alone; each needs the other for its full unfolding. Melody sets the sluggish harmonic masses in motion, for no harmonic progression can be made except through melody—that is, by traversing the intervals. Harmony, on the other hand, connects and organizes the waves of melody.

Since intervals are the stuff of music, every interval must have harmonic and melodic characteristics. Series 2 shows the distribution of these characteristics clearly:

Harmonic force is strongest in the intervals at the beginning of the series, and diminishes towards the end, while melodic force is distributed in just the opposite order. The strongest, most unambiguous interval, after the octave, which is unique, is the fifth, while the most beautiful is the major third, on account of the triad formed by it with its combination tones. From this point on, the harmonic effect decreases, until it nearly disappears in the minor second and major seventh. These two intervals aie of almost exclusively melodic significance, since they form leading-tones. They can receive any considerable harmonic significance only through the simultaneous sounding of other intervals. The simplest melodic step of the minor second is followed, reading from right to left (after the minor seventh), by the strongest and most beautiful melodic interval, the major second. Just as the most beautiful harmonic interval was not at the very beginning of the series, so the chief melodic one does not lie at the very end.

Series 2, exposed to the free play of harmonic and melodic forces, now reveals clearly the weakness of those intervals which have the less favorable disposition of their combination tones, *i. e.*, the inversions of the more favorably arranged ones: they offer less resistance. Harmonic force, which begins at the left, is almost helpless against the melodic strength of the seconds, whereas it is not without effect on the sevenths; on the other hand, melodic force, proceeding from the right, is helpless against the strong third, fifth, and octave. When these intervals occur melodically, that is, one tone after another, they organize even the most fluent line into harmonic groups. Their inversions yield more easily. Strong harmonic intervals exert a powerful attraction, while their inversions become more easily the object of attraction, and so are more likely to perform a melodic function. Thus the major seventh proceeds to the octave, the minor seventh to the sixth, the sixth to the fifth, and, at the left-hand side of the figure, the fourth yields to the attraction of the third. In the sixths, the two forces about balance. Harmonic force is not strong enough always to vanquish the tendency to melodic development—the step to the fifth—, and on the other hand, sixths are not so strong melodically as to demand invariably melodic treatment.

An understanding of these things makes our admiration for mediaeval musical theory greater than ever, for, with all the limitations of its field, and all its clinging to a heritage at odds with musical practice, it always showed an astonishingly sure instinct in all matters pertaining to the intervals. It knew nothing of the power of attraction of the strong intervals, based on the combination tones, and yet it rejected the harmonic interval of the fourth; and it looked with disfavor on melodic leaps of a sixth, not to mention the use of the harmonic intervals of the second and seventh. We are less timid today. We have learned, particularly, to handle sixths either harmonically or melodically, according to the need of the moment, though even today we avoid the harmonic interval of the fourth in places where force and definiteness of expression are desired.

The tritone has no definite significance, either harmonic or melodic. In order to determine its position, we need a third tone. This third tone may sound simultaneously with the tritone,

in which case the tritone is harmonically determined. Or else the tritone may form a part of a group of three successive tones.

When such groups are not mere broken chords (which would be of purely harmonic significance), and when no special means are employed to make the tritone the most important part of the group, it becomes melodically subordinate. One of its two tones becomes the neighboring tone of an interval that is harmonically unambiguous, which then purges the tritone of its indefiniteness.

[89]

The Conventional Theory of Harmony

There are four points in which the conventional theory of harmony appears too narrow a system for the determination and construction of chords:

1. The basic principle for the construction of chords is the superposition of thirds.
2. Chords are considered invertible.
3. By raising or lowering tones of the diatonic scales the chord-supply of a key may be enriched.
4. Chords are susceptible of various interpretations.

As to point 1:

Triads of all species arise from the superposition of thirds, and by the addition of further thirds seventh-chords and ninth-chords are produced. These groups of intervals may be changed, by the rearrangement of their layers, into chords of different degrees of tension. By this simple means, only a small selection from among the possible tonal combinations is made accessible—a selection which includes, to be sure, the best and most useful combinations. But music is caught in a net of which the warp and woof are scales with their inelastic tonal functions and chords with their inversions. Chords that cannot be traced back to a construction in thirds are unexplainable in conventional harmonic theory.

To explain the foregoing simple succession of three-tone chords, which is certainly not at all startling today, the academic theory of harmony has to employ the strangest devices. It may call them appoggiatura-chords or suspension-chords. But here it forgets that an essential part of the appoggiatura or suspension effect is resolution. As long as only the "dissonant" chord is present, and not its resolution, the conditions of an appoggiatura are not fulfilled, and the chords must be looked upon as independent entities. Or it makes the ridiculous assertion that the chords are incomplete, or that they are substitutes for other chords. But who is to decide in each case what parts of the chords are lacking, or for what other chords these are substituting?

As to point 2:

Simple three- and four-tone chords can be rearranged so that their inversions are recognizable as other forms of an original position. That is no longer easy even with ninth chords, and the conventional theory of harmony, in order not to have to burst the bonds of its own rules, chops off parts of these chords in order to fit them into its bed of Procrustes—the inversion system. But the majority of chords, especially those not built up exclusively in thirds, cannot be inverted:

The foregoing formations would lose their character and their sense if their members were rearranged. And we cannot even invert them according to the rules of harmony, since we do not know to what root-tone they are to be related.

As to point 3:

The tonal relations to a basic tone are not exhausted in the tones that belong to the scale of a key. In order to be able to include chords containing tones foreign to the scale of a key without abandoning that key, resort was had to the concept of alteration. Originally conceived to justify a few very common departures from the simplest tonality (such as the lowered sixth degree, and the Neapolitan sixth chord), this idea was expanded to shelter everything else that did not easily fit into the tonal structure, and the result was that such uncertainty and ambiguity were introduced into the system that the only rule that remained valid was: "Any chord can occur in any key." That is the end of the diatonic system; we are now on chromatic ground. In the diatonic system, however, the newly added chords are looked on as subordinate harmonies, almost as unwelcome intruders, whereas in the chromatic system they are considered from the first as independent members of the tonal system.

As to point 4:

If so definite a phenomenon as the dominant seventh chord (taken as a single example of the ambiguity which every chord possesses in harmonic theory) may be interpreted according to function and notation as being either in fundamental or in six-five or in four-three position,

the system is wrong. Of course it would be foolish to say that this chord has the same harmonic significance in all three forms, simply because it sounds the same. Similarly A takes on a different function in the domain of C than in that of F, and what we concede to the individual tone we cannot deny to the chord. Thus we see that in the first of the three resolutions the g^1 is related to the c^1—is in fact its closest relative, as Series 1 shows us. In the second progression it is less closely related to the following root, of which it is the minor second. Naturally, this more distant relationship cannot produce so strong a harmonic step as occurred in the first instance. The third progression, in accordance with the relation of the roots of the two chords, which is what governs, is between the other two in strength: the g^1 ($f\mathbf{x}^1$) is the major third of the following $d\sharp^1$ ($e\flat^1$). From this example we see that the susceptibility of chords to various interpretations is not rooted in sound at all, but springs from the conflict between the acoustic phenomenon and its notation. On the keyboard there is no such ambiguity. Whether a triad is written $d\flat\flat$-$f\flat$-$a\flat\flat$ or $b\sharp$-$d\mathbf{x}$-$f\mathbf{x}$, it is always played on the keys c-e-g, and always sounds so. If we had a tempered notation, there would be only perfect, major, and minor intervals. Augmented and diminished and still more extreme categories would disappear, except in the case of the tritone, which would be the only interval to retain the ambiguity that is indicated by the terms diminished and augmented, and could never be expressed in terms of the normal measures of other intervals. If it is possible to regulate *sound* to the point where the fine interval-gradations disappear between the keys of a tempered keyboard instrument, it should be simpler still to introduce a solution along similar lines into so purely external a medium as notation. Whether this will ever come about, and to what extent it would be possible to reform notation so that it not only would have one symbol for each of the twelve tones, but also would include all the other improvements that are urgently required, we need not consider here. So long as we continue to use the double notation in sharps and flats, we must of course insist on the most logical and consistent notation of musical phenomena, just as in reproducing the spoken language in writing or in print we stick to the traditional spellings, and continue to use the spelling "sh", for example, while other systems of writing, such as the Cyrillic, or the phonetic, employ much simpler and clearer symbols.

Our somewhat complicated system of musical notation has the advantage of giving the singer or the player (especially of untempered instruments) in most cases a clear impression of the melodic or harmonic intentions of the composer. For analysis of the sound itself, on the other hand, it is not only worthless but actually a hindrance. For in such analysis our thesis must be that all intervals and chords are perceived, independently of their notation, as the ear first hears them, without reference to what has gone before or what comes after. The ear does not hesitate, in the course of this perception, between making all the necessary calculations of minute interval-differences, on the one hand, and, on the other, applying to each chord or interval the measurements derived from the simplest proportions of the overtone series. It always adopts the latter course, and hears every interval, even such as do not actually fit, as being of about the size of one of the intervals that we know from our two series. An interval whose tones stand only roughly in the proportions 5:6 is always heard by the ear as a minor third, whether it is written and intended by the composer as an augmented second, a minor third, or a doubly diminished fourth. Aural

[93]

analysis thus takes account of no diminished or augmented intervals except the tritone; it hears all other intervals as forms of the intervals derived from the first six tones of the overtone series.

Now this thesis will seem to many musicians an aberration based on crass materialism. But when they examine their objections closely, they will find that the only support for these objections is in notation—and notation, as we have said, is not to be touched. Apart from their love of correct notation, however, they are by no means so fastidious, for they mostly do not hesitate to use the piano in their teaching of harmony, and that instrument takes no heed of their desire for functional accuracy. They should find food for thought also in the fact that in listening to music on untempered instruments (choruses, string quartets, orchestras, etc.) they would always be faced with the question of just which of the various interval-sizes to apply in each case, unless they knew the notation or their ears were kind enough to take care of the question independently. Even the hypersensitive ear goes through this same process of normalization in the perception of intervals, and it is well that this is so, for to an ear that analyzed every harmonic phenomenon with complete accuracy we should not be able to offer any usable tonal system. We should stand helpless before an incomprehensible world of tone. Thus we may recognize in our ability to accept complex intervals as versions of their nearest simple equivalents a friendly gift of nature that makes life bearable for the musical ear, as does for the spirit the ability to forget, and for the body the capacity for accustoming oneself to pain.

10

Chord Analysis

(See the table at the end of this book)

The requirements of a new system of chord analysis follow from our criticism of the conventional theory of harmony.

1. Construction in thirds must no longer be the basic rule for the erection of chords.

2. We must substitute a more all-embracing principle for that of the invertibility of chords.
3. We must abandon the thesis that chords are susceptible of a variety of interpretations.

Although all the chords that may be used in music must be covered by our new system in a clear and easily understandable order, it will not completely upset the theses of accepted harmonic theory. Despite the required basic changes, we shall make no such alterations within the relatively small domain covered by the chord analysis of the familiar theory of harmony that a stranger, wandering into our new structure, would be entirely lost. The ground-plan of the old building remains; it has simply been incorporated into a much larger one. The new structure must thus be regarded as a great and timely extension.

As to point 1:

We define a chord as a group of at least three different tones sounding simultaneously. Two tones do not form a chord, no matter how often they are doubled in any number of octaves; they form only an interval. The principle which is to replace that of the superposition of thirds as the basis for chord erection we derive from Series 2, and from the root effect connected with one tone of every interval. This principle will be clearest without a great deal of explanation and description if we approach it indirectly: We shall examine the nature of various kinds of chords, in order to deduce from them the means of synthesis.

At the beginning and end of Series 2, separated from the pairs of intervals, we have the octave and the tritone. The octave has no significance for chord analysis, since all it can do is to increase the weight of one tone of an interval, by doubling, without making any essential change in the content of the interval. The tritone, on the other hand, stamps chords so strongly with its own character that they acquire something of both its indefiniteness and its character of motion towards a goal. There thus arises an essential difference between chords containing a tritone and those without one; and our sense of the stability of chords and intervals thus divides the entire chordal material into two groups: Group A includes all chords that have no tritone; Group B includes all chords containing a tritone.

If we appraise the intervals of Series 2 according to the degrees of relationship of Series 1, the five pairs of intervals will divide into two classes: those consisting of the first-generation descendants of the progenitor tone (fifths, fourths, thirds, and sixths) and those formed from the "grandchildren" (seconds and sevenths). This classification enables us to make a subdivision of the chords in Groups A and B. For if we construct chords using the intervals belonging to the first of these classifications only, it follows that such chords, owing to the simplicity and purity of their constituents, must form one division, the chords of which will be simpler and purer than those containing seconds or sevenths, which form the second division. About these we shall have more to say later.

Now as to the third factor that must be taken into consideration in our judgement of chords: the root, and its position in the chord. Chords consist of intervals, and since in each interval one of the tones is the root and dominates the other, the interval-roots try to bring other tones under their control, and to exert their dominance in the chord as well as in their own intervals. Every chord, then, with a few exceptions to be mentioned later, has a root. To find it, we must find the best interval of the chord, appraised according to the values of Series 2: the fifth is the best, the major seventh the weakest of harmonic intervals (except for the tritone). For our calculation, we must take into account every interval in the chord. A major triad thus consists of a fifth, a major third, and a minor third. Here we see the difference between our method and that of the conventional theory of harmony, which relates the chord factors to the bass tone, a process which makes inversions possible. But at the same time it reckons with the intervals of the uninverted,

[96]

fundamental position of the chord, so that the root remains the same in all inversions, and the other tones of the original position also retain their original functions in the inverted position. This double reckoning is inaccurate; there can be but one basis of calculation if misunderstandings are to be avoided. We say, on the other hand: if there is a fifth in the chord, then the lower tone of the fifth is the root of the chord. Similarly, the lower tone of a third or a seventh (in the absence of any better interval) is the root of the chord. Conversely, if a fourth, or a sixth, or a second is the best interval of a chord, then its upper tone is the root of the chord. Doubled tones count only once; we use the lowest one for our reckoning. If the chord contains two or more equal intervals, and these are the best intervals, the root of the lower one is the root of the chord.

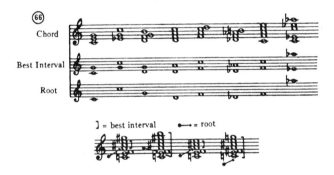

It makes no difference whether the tone that completes the best interval lies in the same octave or one or more octaves higher (in fifths, thirds, and sevenths) or, on the other hand, one or more octaves lower (in fourths, sixths, and seconds). In those occasional instances in which the compass of the whole chord is so great that the distance between the two tones of the root-determining interval permits the formation of "dissonant" combination tones such as were mentioned earlier, in the discussion of separate intervals (pp. 72–4), we have the choice either of making new rules or of simply treating the widely extended intervals like their closer prototypes.

[97]

Here, too, I hold it unnecessary to set up special rules to govern these few exceptions, instead of applying to the latter the rules that hold in the great majority of cases. We may therefore without hesitation treat extended intervals like those of Fig. 66[a] as fifths, fourths, etc., and accordingly assume the roots of these chords to be C, c^2, G_1, C, and $B\flat_1$.

In such unusual chord arrangements as

it would usually be better to take melodic influences (such as will be discussed later) into account, rather than to rely exclusively upon harmonic analysis. These chords would then become subordinate to others more easily analyzed, so that either the roots which our rules would lead us to deduce (b^2 and f^3, for the chords of Fig. 67) would be confirmed by their context, or else the more effective roots of the predominant chords would make the analysis of the formations here notated unnecessary.

As to point 2:

In the conventional theory of harmony, the inversion of a chord never has the same strong and definite effect as the chord had in its original position. For in the fundamental position the root and bass tone are the same; the root, already the strongest tone of the chord, is further strengthened by its position at the bottom of the

[98]

chord. In inversions the two forces are separated; the root is now in an upper part of the chord, and opposing its strength to that of the bass. Strictly speaking, it is not the rearrangement of the tones of a chord that constitutes an inversion, but the transposition of its root into an upper part. Hitherto the fact that one chord (an inversion) had to be related to another chord, of different structure (the original position, in which the root and the bass tone were the same), has prevented a comprehensive use of the principle of root-transposition. By freeing this principle from its fetters, we gain not only a wider view over the domain of numerous chords not hitherto covered by harmonic theory, but also a new criterion for the appraisal of chords. All chords in which the bass tone and the root are not identical are subordinate to chords whose other characteristics (root and chord-group qualities) they share, but in which the root and bass tone do coincide. Here, too, we do not care whether the interval which determines the root lies in the closest position in the chord, or whether its tones are spread out over one or more octaves. There is, it is true, a difference in the sound and in the value of chords in which the root is emphasized by the close proximity of the tones of the intervals which determine it, as compared with those in which the root is weakened by being widely separated from its partner. But if we were to take account of these subtlest differences we should not be able to erect any practical system, since each tonal combination would have to have its own individual niche. The division here proposed may, however, despite the sacrifice of excessive subdivisions of sufficient accuracy, be accepted as a basis for the complete understanding of all chords, as will be seen when the picture is complete.

There is a kind of rearrangement of chord-tones which is not to be regarded as inversion, since it does not affect the root tone—which remains stationary—but simply transposes its complementary tone (perhaps with other chord tones) into a different octave. This is a change of what the accepted theory of harmony calls *position* ("close", "open", "mixed", "position of the octave", "fifth", "third", etc.). The ranking of the chords in the following example is the same whether they appear in form A or form B,

since it follows from what has been said that the increased distance between the root and its complement, despite the slight change in effect which results from it, does not affect the values we assign to the chords. This closing up or spreading out of the chord-tones is not possible in all combinations. Chords which, owing to their simple structure, possess only a mild tension are not greatly altered by such changes. But chords containing many tones lose their particular character when they undergo such changes of position. Exactly where the boundary lies between these two types of chords can be decided only in each individual instance.

As to point 3:

The division of chords into two main groups (A and B), the members of which are then further ranked according to their component intervals and the position of their roots, does away with all ambiguity. It does not, of course, abolish the harmonic uncertainty of the tritone. But anyone who considers this a failing should balance the uncertainty of a few chords against the inaccuracy of a system in which any chord may have a different meaning from that which the ear assigns to it.

As a matter of experience it is established that the tritone, when combined with other intervals to form a chord, subordinates itself to the best interval of Series 2. The intervals of the first two pairs (fifth and fourth, major third and minor sixth) do away with its uncertainty, but yield readily to its tendency towards a resolution. Thus it happens that in tritone chords containing these intervals the root is just as strong as it is in the chords of Group A, but stability is nevertheless lacking.

The intervals of the next pair (minor third and major sixth) have less strength to combat the uncertainty of the tritone and thus to make of it a clear harmonic combination:

Thus a chord which apart from the tritone possesses only a minor third or a major sixth remains as ambiguous as the tritone itself. Just as in the tritone itself, one of the tones of such a chord will be called the *root representative*. The contextual chord-succession determines which of the tones performs this function. There are only four such chords: the diminished triad with its two inversions and the diminished seventh chord.

Among the chords which have no tritone, also, there are two of which the interpretation depends on the context:

and which in consequence have no root, but only a root representative: the augmented triad and the chord composed of two superposed fourths.

11

Subdivision of the Chord-Groups

Within each of the two main Groups, A (without tritone) and B (with tritone), three subdivisions may be made, according to the principles already discussed. We shall label them with Roman numerals, so that Group A contains the sub-groups I, III, and V, while Group B contains II, IV, and VI.

Sub-group I of Group A contains chords having no seconds or sevenths, and in its first section (I_1) only those in which the root and the bass tone coincide—in which, that is, the best interval is based on the bottom tone. There are but two chords that fulfill these conditions: the major and minor triads. These noblest of all chords constitute a section in themselves. They alone are completely independent, capable of being used for conclusions, and of being connected with any other chords. The chords of the next section (I_2) stand a little lower in the scale of values. These are the chords in which the root is not the lowest tone: the inversions of the major and minor triads. On account of the high position of the root, they are not independent enough to form satisfying conclusions; but otherwise they perform in somewhat weaker fashion the same functions as those of the preceding section. All the chords of these two sections are at most three-voiced; any additional tones can only be doublings of tones already present. These chords exhaust the possibilities of combining the intervals consisting of the tones most closely related to the progenitor tone (the "sons") in Series 1.

The corresponding sub-group of Group B (II), contains the chords of three or more voices in which the tritone is subordinate to stronger intervals. The requirement that the chords must contain no seconds or sevenths cannot be maintained here, for the presence of the tritone always (except in the diminished triad and its inversions) involves seconds or sevenths. Yet in this sub-group we shall limit ourselves to *major* seconds and *minor* sevenths, as the less sharp representatives of their species. The mildest form of the intensification brought about by the presence of the tritone is the minor seventh, in a chord from which the major second, as the stronger and sharper of the two intervals, still remains excluded; the chord's stability is ensured by the coinciding of the bass tone with the root. In this section (IIa) we thus find only the two most important tritone chords: the complete dominant seventh, and the same chord without fifth. The chords in which the major second as well as the minor seventh may appear fall into three sections. The first (IIb_1) includes those chords in which the root and the bass tone are the same: the strong dominant chords which are the next simplest after the dominant seventh, and which in their structure lean heavily upon the chords of their neighboring section (I_1), the triads. The second section (IIb_2) contains the chords in which the root is not at the bottom: the inversions of simple dominant chords

[102]

and similar structures. Common to all the chords of sub-group II thus far named is the fact that they contain only one tritone. The chords of the third section (IIb₃) are similar in every respect but this: they contain two or even three tritones. These chords are not included in the foregoing sections because their sound is so strongly colored by the tritones; yet they are not so intensified as to require assignment to sub-group IV.

Sub-group III of Group A contains chords of any number of tones which are extended by the addition of seconds or sevenths. These are a rough and unpolished race. The best of them are those with three or four tones, which either contain one of the chords of sub-group I, or at least in some of their tones approach this un-attainable prototype very closely. And the chords that lack minor seconds and major sevenths (*i. e.,* those limiting themselves to major seconds and minor sevenths) are of a higher class than the very sharp and grating ones which contain these intervals. None of the chords of sub-group III are independent; all of them depend very much on the course of melody; and they cannot be connected with all other chords. They include the secondary seventh-chords with their inversions. The first section again contains only those in which the root is in the bass; the second section contains those in which the root is in a higher part.

Sub-group IV contains a strange set of piquant, coarse, and highly colored chords. All the chords that serve the most intensified ex-pression, that make a noise, that irritate, stir the emotions, ex-cite strong aversion—all are at home here. The chords of this group can have any number of tritones, and the number of minor seconds and major sevenths is likewise unlimited. It would be unreasonable to expect chords of such strongly marked individuality to lend themselves without resistance to all chord-successions, as do triads and the simpler tritone chords. They are often very intractable, especially when they are used in progressions involving chords from various and rapidly changing sub-groups. The best of them are the easiest to handle—those that consist of only a few tones and that resemble chords of the simpler sub-groups.

Sub-groups V and VI are small. They contain the above mentioned uncertain chords—chords consisting of several superposed intervals of the same size. The first chord of sub-group V consists of two major thirds and an augmented fifth. The augmented fifth can be counted a minor sixth, in accordance with what we have already established, and thus the constituents of the chord belong to the same pair of intervals, and the root cannot be definitely determined. The chord built up in fourths, which belongs to group V, may occur in forms in which its root can be determined. It is uncertain only in its closest position (see the table), or when its highest tone is doubled above or its lowest below, or when the outer tones are spread an octave further apart and there is an octave doubling of the middle tone between them (c^1 f^1 f^2 bb^2). Any other doublings produce a fifth as the best interval of the chord, which would place it in sub-group III. The same is true even when it consists of only three tones, expanded or contracted by the octave transposition of one of them. If we add further fourths above, we had better assume the presence of a root, for the choice of possible root representatives becomes too great. Accordingly we shall treat all chords consisting of three or more superposed fourths as having the root of their lowest fourth as the chord-root. Two superposed fifths do not belong to group V but to group III; likewise two superposed major or minor seconds. Chords consisting of two or more superposed minor thirds constitute group VI.

For handling the chords of Group B (those with tritone), it is not enough to know their roots. If we are to be able to make convincing chord-progressions, we must treat the tritone as their most important constituent. We find the root by the familiar method. But, in addition, one of the members of the tritone must serve as the *guide-tone*. To find the guide-tone, the following rules apply:

1. That tone belonging to one or more tritones in the chord which stands in the best relationship to the root (measured by the interval-values of Series 2) is to be considered the guide-tone:

In doubtful cases—as for example, when a choice must be made

[104]

between two tones which lie above and below the root and are equally related to it—let that tone be taken as guide-tone which, itself a part of a tritone, leads best to the root of the next chord (if that chord has no tritone) or to the guide-tone of the next chord (if it contains a tritone).

2. When there is only one tritone in the chord, and the root forms a part of this tritone, the other tone forming the tritone is to be considered the guide-tone.

When isolated intervals appear between one chord and the next, they are to be regarded as belonging to that group to which their own nature would assign them. The fifth and the thirds belong to I_1, the fourth and the sixths to I_2, the seconds to III_2, the sevenths to III_1, the tritone to VI.

This system of appraising chords and intervals results in a classification of *all* chords. There is no combination of intervals which does not fit into some division of our system. Chords which a theorist would analyze only in his nightmares, and which any self-respecting counterpoint book would not tolerate, can now be easily explained.

The system is as comprehensive as it can be, in view of the possible variety of chords. Nevertheless, even by this system, there will always remain a certain number of exceptional chords which cannot be interpreted with complete satisfaction. These include those which consist of so many different tones that the individual units of which the structure is composed hardly count, as well as those which, although they contain only a few tones, are so spread out that their constituent tones can only with difficulty be perceived as constituting harmonic intervals. But it is a question whether a system of investigation which aims to make clear the harmonic side of tonal combinations should be applied to chords which, like the first-named, are effective chiefly through their intensity, their mass, or their energy, or, like the second group, result simply from the isolated effect of single tones or lines. An investigation of these border-line cases will, however, produce an easy *modus vivendi* with such structures.

12

The Value of Chords

The complete material of the conventional theory of harmony is contained in our sub-groups I, II, and VI, except for an isolated chord here and there belonging to groups III and IV. And, of course, all possible chords may occur under conventional harmonic theory, but it accepts them only as structures resulting from strong melodic tendencies, and it interprets all tones that complicate chords beyond the familiar limits of triads and seventh chords as passing tones, suspensions, appoggiature, etc. When one of the chords belonging to our groups III or IV shows an urge for independent existence, and cannot be explained as consisting of appoggiature or suspensions or passing tones, it is considered simply as non-existent. There is no room in a well-ordered household for such rabble; they had better be chased from the door, before one is tempted to examine them more closely.

In another way, too, the familiar theory of harmony prevents chords from the free unfolding of their vital urge. For it proclaims as the highest harmonic law the relationship of tones and chords in a key. The diatonic scale with its limited possibilities determines the position and rank of the chords, which are the mere satellites of this power. The chord must blindly subordinate itself, and attention be paid to its individual character only as the key allows. This theory of harmony is like an employer who keeps a small number of gifted and versatile artisans at work. They are tied to him for better or for worse, and he has always kept them so dependent upon him that they are no longer capable of making their own decisions. Therefore he places a supervisor over them, who plans and thinks for them. The work of such men will never rise above a certain quality, since the directing personality is not omniscient and not equally well prepared at all times and for every contingency, since work which is not free cannot develop beyond a

CHAPTER IV

Harmony

1

Movement in Chord-Successions

We have seen that the individual tone is useful for musical purposes only as a result of the interval between it and another tone. Similarly, a chord, which is an aggregation of tones, has musical significance only when the appearance of another harmonic aggregation creates a space between them. The spanning of this gap—chord-connection—is the beginning of all harmonic reality. Thus in the realm of chords the procedure is the same, on a higher level, as that through which the simplest of all tonal building units acquired its significance: the creation of tension by the juxtaposition of two entities.

Three forces are at work in chord-connection: rhythmic, melodic, and harmonic. Each of them works in two directions. Rhythm determines the duration of the chords, and groups them by division into stressed and unstressed members of the structure. Melody in *voice-leading* regulates linear expansion, and in the *two-voice framework* sets the pitch limits. In the *placing of the harmonic center of gravity* and in the regulation of *relationships* we see harmonic energy at work.

We can leave the function of rhythm out of consideration here, but not because it is unimportant. Without rhythm—that is, without relationships in time—neither of the other forces could operate. It is rather the all-pervading force of the primeval element of rhythm that allows us to take it for granted, and to simplify our work by ignoring it. Furthermore, all questions of rhythm, as well as of the formal characteristics of composition which spring from it, are still so largely unexplained that it seems impossible at the present time to include rhythm as an integral part of a system of teaching the craft of composition. In this work, which does not aim at the complete scientific explanation of the deepest impulses that underlie musical writing, but rather seeks to be of practical use, we shall limit ourselves to the examination of the other forces. Whereas rhythm can find expression without relation to the tones and chords—in fact, without relation to sound itself—these other elements, in order to make themselves felt, must behave according to the laws which we have come to know in Series 1 and Series 2. They thus form a coherent group, different from and counter-balancing the rhythmic element. We are limiting our field of investigation by excluding from it on the one hand the primary musical elements—pitch, intensity, and timbre—and rhythm, and on the other hand the forces of dynamics, phrasing, and agogics, which of course affect chord-connections but do not change them.

The special characteristics of melodic structures will be discussed in Chapter V. Still, we must treat the subject of *voice-leading* at this point in our discussion at least sufficiently to explain its workings in harmonic connections. In one type of musical writing, the form and content of the piece is determined by melodic force: this is contrapuntal writing. When, on the other hand, the *chords* and their connections are what give the piece its character, melody is of less significance.

Between the extreme of linear writing and a texture so thoroughly chordal in purpose there are innumerable species of the mutual interpenetration of melodic and harmonic forces. What determines our assigning of a composition to one or the other domain is not so much the external appearance as the basic attitude of the piece. In contrapuntal writing the composer takes the idea of movement as his point of departure, and the chords come about as the product of the play of line (although this product itself must have its own logic)—they form the adhesive which *binds* these lines *together*. In chordal writing, the composer sets out with the opposite idea: he

[110]

breaks up the inert chord masses and breathes life into them by dividing their components among moving voices. The binding together of the flowing lines may be so firm, and the breaking up of the chord masses may set so much movement free, that a music in which the most alive linear movement is combined with the most logical harmonic progression can hardly be classed as primarily one thing or the other. In an idiom employing really independent voices, every tone of one chord moves to a tone of the next, while in a more compact idiom (such as in keyboard writing) no such melodic progression of the individual tones is sought, and it is rather chords that are juxtaposed, in whole or in part. Thus harmonic masses are set into flowing motion by melodic means of progression, on the one hand by the aggregation of individual movements of tones, and on the other by the shifting of entire chord-structures (see also Chapter III, Section 8).

In well balanced progressions involving really independent voices, all melodic steps are of great (though not of equally great) importance. It is not true, as many a theorizing aesthete would have us believe, that the voices are absolutely free to move as they choose, and that the chordal aspect may then be left to assume whatever shape it will. To leave the harmonic dimension, which after rhythm and melody is the most important element of music, to chance—would this not be like planning only the horizontal parts of a building? Whether the architect is building a tower or a shed, he cannot escape vertical as well as horizontal elements. He can emphasize one element, and thus subordinate the other, but he cannot wholly exclude either one. In music, too, no matter how much attention is focused on the melodic lines, the harmonic aspect cannot be ignored. If it has no logical relation to the linear texture, and if it is not in itself logically developed, the music is unpalatable.

There is, of course, another linear style of writing from which, despite the convincing nature of the harmonic progression, we derive no satisfaction. Here independence has been pushed too far: every voice has such a strong and independent life of its own that the net result is a maze of activity that is difficult to understand;

rhythm and harmony can no longer impose unity on the various melodic personalities which insist on going their own way. Just as one cannot handle six different kinds of things at the same time, so one cannot follow a large number of independent voices; one's attention is torn hither and thither, and it takes account at each instant only of the most prominent point from among the tangled lines, subordinating the rest. Even two very independent and conflicting lines are hard to follow, unless they are bound together by a fairly simple harmonic foundation. When there are three voices, none of them is completely free in its spatial (melodic) aspect; therefore in skilful three-part writing one of the three voices is always subordinated to the other two. The significance of the voices, their prominence or lack of it, may change within time units less than one beat long. In contrapuntal writing for more than three voices, the relative prominence given to the voices needs even more care; here the sustaining of individual tones, the parallel coupling of voices, and the emphasis of the harmonic content bring about numerous gradations, of which the fugues of Bach furnish the most perfect examples.

Contrapuntal writing does not satisfy all demands. It is found lacking particularly by those players and hearers who seek in music more sweetness and gracefulness, as well as a greater display of force and a more immediate effect than the cool strength and logic of independent lines can produce. Writing which is primarily chordal and homophonic sacrifices the multiplicity of lines, and can accordingly allow to its small linear ingredient, which rests upon the chords as the wave does upon the waters, a freer and more sensuous development. What is important here is the exact fitting of the main harmonic components, and the strength of these easily carries the weight of the less important element; in fact, it carries much incidental and often even much superfluous material as well. The play of line may become so weakened that it can hardly be observed at all; music in which this happens runs the risk of utter futility, or of the same incomprehensibility that attends counterpoint pushed to dogmatic lengths. Incomprehensibility is the result also of too rapid changes of chord, of continual use of the sharpest combinations (those belonging to sub-groups III and IV), and of inaccurate or obscure harmonic progressions. The danger of becoming unintelligible is greater in contrapuntal writing; the chordal style is more liable to sink into shallow insignificance.

2

The Two-Voice Framework

In both the contrapuntal and the chordal idioms, harmonic development, which is tied to melodic movement, takes place within an external spatial frame—a skeleton which gives the chords the necessary contour. This framework is constructed by the bass voice and the most important of the upper voices. The bass line may be clearly melodic in character, as in contrapuntal writing, or it may hardly rise above connecting the main points of harmonic support, but it will always have, as the lowest voice and the foundation of the structure, decisive importance for the development of the harmony. The next most important line may in contrapuntal writing be entrusted to any one of the upper voices; or, since the voices perform functions of constantly varying importance, it may move about from voice to voice. In the chordal idiom, it will always be found in the "theme" or the "melody", or whatever one wishes to call the linear formation that floats above the chords. Usually this is the highest stratum in the tonal composite; less often it is embedded in the middle of the chords. If the melodic aspect is so obscured by the rhythm or the harmony that one can hardly speak of any thematic coherence, then the upper voice that results from the chord-successions takes its place. If the bass voice holds an organ point, then the next higher moving voice constitutes the lower half of the framework, although one must be sure that the organ point really leaves the harmony free to develop, and does not have a disturbing significance of its own. For when the organ point becomes a constituent of the harmony (even though only in passing), it loses its organ-point function and is reckoned as part of the harmony. Similarly, when the upper voice holds a tone for some time, the next lower voice becomes the upper member of the framework.

[113]

If writing in several voices is to sound clear and intelligible, the contours of its two-voice framework must be cleanly designed and cogently organized. The bass voice must make with the most important of the upper voices, regardless of the difference in register between them, a good, intelligible piece of two-part writing, needing nothing further to complete it. The two voices must not interfere with each other, as they easily may if each is made to bear too much melodic weight; rather must they be contrasted and balanced one against the other, in their shape and in their time-values. This two-part framework is no mere scaffolding to assist the composer in his work; it is a living member of the body of the musical work. Thus it must not be limited to the form of a meaningless two-part counterpoint exercise, note against note. Yet it must also not assume such importance as to reduce the other elements of the piece to insignificance, for despite its importance it is only one part of the tonal structure.

The intervals formed by the two voices must be carefully planned. Thirds and sixths are pleasant intervals, but to construct a two-part texture mainly of them would be to bore the listener with continual sweetness. Seconds and sevenths add strength and tension to two-part writing; yet their continuous use would dull the ear and make it insensible to the subtler charms of the more satisfactory intervals. Thus a combination of euphony and sharpness of sound must be found, appropriate to the nature and purpose of the composition. Tensions and relaxations must alternate. But there is no place here in the Theoretical Part of this work for specific rules governing two-part writing; such rules will be found in the later volumes.

The progression of the two-voice framework is wholly independent of the other tones of the chords. To be sure, these other tones belong to the whole tonal picture just as much as the outlines themselves, but they have no more influence on the latter than the form of the spleen or the liver has on the external appearance of a man. Already in examining the nature of the individual chord we saw that the tones that filled it up, and their close or extended position, did not have the same significance as the position of the chord in space determined by the position of its root. In chord-progressions, then, since they are composed of individual chords, these filling-in tones are also of secondary importance. The path of a chord in space is affected only very little by the inner tones; its shape is determined rather by melodic progression, principally in the form of the two-voice framework. It is in the harmonic relations of the chords, and especially in the shifting of the center of harmonic gravity, that the inner voices play their full rôle.

In the polyphony of all ages and styles this two-voice framework will be found, tracing the spatial boundaries of the harmony. As the contour of the chords it acts as a constant reminder not to allow spots of harmonic color to become so gorgeous as to obscure the drawing itself; it is at the same time, however, like a rudimentary organ that remains in the human body as a heritage from some evolutionary ancestor, an honorable legacy from the dawn of polyphony, a relic of which we can no more free ourselves than we can of such atavistic parts of the body.

3

Harmonic Fluctuation

A solid object—a brick, for example—can be pushed or pulled in such a way that its under side remains in uninterrupted contact with the surface on which it rests. But it can also be turned over on its side, or even moved violently enough to turn on one of its corners. In this case we have added to change of position a turning of the object on its own axis, resulting from a shift in its center of gravity. The brick then touches the ground with first one surface and then another. The first of these types of movement corresponds to the harmonic progression in which the relations of all the roots to their respective chords is governed by the same principle—as when none but chords belonging to a single sub-group (I_1 or I_2, III_1, etc.) are used. The second type corresponds to the shift of harmonic gravity; for this we shall henceforth use the term *harmonic fluctuation*.

If we look at the sub-groups of our chord-table—say, at group

I—, we shall see that the chords of the two sections I_1 and I_2 are differentiated by the position of their roots. The chords of I_2 are in what the conventional theory of harmony calls inversion: they have been turned side over side or end over end, so that they are lying on their sides or standing on their heads, while the chords of I_1 stand firmly on their feet. Now, we have already seen that there is a difference in value between the chords of these two sections: those of the first section are, because of their strong root-positions, higher in value than the less stable chords of the second. If in a chord-succession a chord of the first section is followed by one of the second, there results, as we have seen, a decrease in value. The step from a more valuable to a less valuable chord is in the harmonic sense, then, a descent, a fall, and conversely a step from a less valuable to a more valuable one is an ascent. But since in our chord-table the harmonic *tension* of chords *increases* from section to section and from sub-group to sub-group in the same proportion as the *value decreases*, the progression from a higher to a lower chord represents an increase in tension, and a step in the opposite direction a decrease. It is this up-and-down change of values and tensions which we shall term harmonic fluctuation. This fluctuation may be gradual or sudden according to the relative values of the chords which make up the progression. In progressions from I_1 to III_2, or from IIb_1 to IV_2, or the reverse, the ascent or descent may be regarded as sudden, because the value-differences are great; here the brick turns side over side or end over end and traverses a good deal of space. Progressions within one sub-group, on the other hand, as for example from IIa to IIb_3, or from III_2 to III_1, may be considered gradual.

To create any harmonic fluctuation, chords of different value are always needed, be the difference ever so slight: as for example between two chords both belonging to section III_1, of which one resembles the chords of group I more closely than the other, and so stands slightly higher in the scale of values. Harmonic fluctuation is thus not to be confused with the scale of harmonic values which results from relationships within a key. Such relationships can give different significance to chords of the same structure and value: our brick is placed together with other identical bricks, and receives its particular significance from its relative position in the building. In the connection of chords of identical structure there is no harmonic fluctuation; there are only harmonic relations which vary and together with the rhythmic pulse regulate the tonal movement and build forms out of it.

The foregoing may be made clearer through the following examples.* In the first example we see six harmonies all belonging to Group A:

Degree of Tension I_1 I_2 I_2 III_2 I_2 I_1

The first and last of these harmonies, belonging to section I_1, are the best and most satisfying, while between them a harmonic development takes place which passes through two chords of I_2, one of III_2, and one of I_2 again. Thus there is an increase of tension from the first chord to the fourth, which is then resolved. The harmonic fluctuation is here not very sudden. The greatest gap is between I_1 and III_2, and this gap is smoothly bridged by the I_2 chords. There is a harmonic *crescendo* and *diminuendo* that is indissolubly connected with the nature of this progression; it cannot be altered by the performer. It is thus different from purely dynamic increases and decreases, the control of which always rests with the singer or player.

The fluctuation in the next example is less smooth:

I_1 III_2 III_1 III_2 III_2 III_1 I_1

* The drawings are intended to give an approximate picture of the changing tension in the musical examples. Beneath the chords of I_1, which are altogether lacking in tension, the upper and lower lines of the diagram come together, while the point of greatest tension corresponds to the widest separation of these lines.

Between the first chord and the second, the gradient, so to speak, is very steep. The highly tense chords of group III give the rest of this progression its character, while the fluctuation among them is not very wide, rising and falling between III_1 and III_2. Of all these chords, the fourth is the sharpest, its minor second (or ninth) e^1-f^2 exceeding in this respect the major seconds and minor sevenths of its neighbors. Between the next to the last chord and the last one there is again an important change of level, which gives the effect of a considerable relaxation of tension. The next two examples

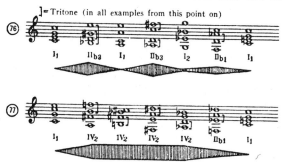

contain chords from Group B (with tritone), the first example restricting itself to the harmless ones of group II, while the second one employs the more biting combinations of group IV. The nature of the harmonic fluctuation will doubtless be clear to the reader with the help of the numbering and the diagrams.

For anyone with some knowledge of the devices of the technique of composition, consideration of harmonic fluctuation introduces no new difficulty, particularly since the conventional theory of harmony takes account of it, even though only to a slight degree: division of chords into those in root position and those in inversion is nothing else. Conventional harmonic theory does not provide, of course, any key to the construction of complicated designs of fluctuating tension; for this we must employ our detailed knowledge of chord-values. Whoever possesses such knowledge can create harmonic structures of the most daring thrust and tension without having to rely on the uncertain method of trying out each individual combination by ear—a process that soon becomes more a guessing game in pursuit of concealed possibilities than a form of creative work. We thus add to the time-honored practices of harmony—voice-leading, and the production of tonal relations—the observation of the rise and fall of harmonic tension as an exact and completely reliable procedure. Since this procedure adds to the accuracy of our planning and execution of harmonic structures, the composer may unhesitatingly accept the added work which this increased material brings with it. The secret of good arrangement of this rise and fall is completely open to him in our table of the chord-values.

The only rule we must observe which involves consideration of individual cases is to remember that the indeterminate chords of groups V and VI introduce an element of uncertainty into harmonic developments. When one is dealing with chords belonging to the other sub-groups, one stands on firm ground; but the introduction of the indeterminate chords is like a step into mud and quicksand. Usually a progression to such a chord represents a decrease in value and accordingly an increase in tension, as our chord-table shows. But sometimes the effect of the use of chords of groups V and VI is such that the whole progression takes on a wavering unsteadiness. The ear still perceives changes of value and tension, but it cannot determine the exact degrees of these changes. In such progressions, therefore, care must be exercised. A single step into uncertainty may be very pleasant, for variety's sake, but a progression consisting exclusively of uncertain chords is always of poor effect. In such a progression we lose all sense of direction; we seem to be tossed aimlessly hither and yon on an endless series of waves until the ear becomes confused to the point of actual physical discomfort. As a counterpoise to the stable and tensionless chords of group I, a chord from group V or VI may be useful; it can almost always be successfully juxtaposed even against chords from group II. But in using it with chords from groups III and IV, care must be exercised. In the midst of such chords, a chord of group V or VI often puts us completely off the track; it seems to cause the whole chord-structure to collapse. Probably the vagueness which results from the complex, over-sharp profiles of the chords of groups III and IV is unsatisfactory when associated with the opposite type of vagueness, which results from the washed-out ambiguity of those of groups V and VI. Progressions of this type must accordingly be handled with extreme care, if they are not to be entirely inconsistent with the rest of the harmonic development.

I can imagine that to a reader who is thoroughly entangled in earlier ways of harmonic thinking the measurement of the harmonic fluctuation will seem an unnecessary addition to the composer's task. And not improbably even some readers who have accepted all the innovations and extensions suggested so far will look on this one as mere hair-splitting, instead of as a logical part of our system. Perhaps both types of readers will be convinced of its necessity by examining the following progression:

The theory of harmony has no place for any of these chords except the first and last. It admits only that the example is in a poor sort of C major. But even our reckoning of the roots tells us nothing more than that all the chords have the same root, c^1. Since, however, they are, despite that fact, quite different from one another, we must expand our analysis by the addition of another criterion. The mere movement of the tones tells us only that against a constant center, consisting of two voices sustaining their tones, two lines are set in contrary motion (the upper one in parallel fourths), reaching their widest compass in the fourth chord. In the two-voice framework we see a unison expanding through a major third and a minor sixth until it too reaches its widest span, a minor seventh, in the fourth chord; and then, after the minor third, the indeterminate tritone before the end introducing an element of uncertainty into the progression. Only in the harmonic fluctuation have we an explanation for the varying harmonic tension of different chords upon the same root. We see there that after a sharp ascent from I_1

to III_2, the third chord brings a further slight increase in tension, which is somewhat relaxed in the fourth chord, containing no minor second. The high point of harmonic tension is in the next to the last chord. Thus the harmonic fluctuation has a quite different development from that of the voice-leading or of the two-voice framework. In this simple example we see the interlocking play of the structural elements quite clearly. The more carefully these elements are balanced, the more convincing, the more interesting, and the more attractive a harmonic progression will be. The purpose of the progressions, the intensity with which they are to affect the hearer, must always determine the coinciding or contrasting designs of all the different elements.

4

Movement in Chord-Connection, Expressed in Root-Progressions

In harmonic fluctuation we see how chords compare with one another as tonal masses of particular forms and densities. We know that the chords are placed in reciprocal relations by means of voice-leading. We need no reminder that in these relations even the most incidental tonal constituent cannot be left to chance. The composer must find for every chord and every tone the treatment that will best reconcile his artistic intention with the nature of his material. For the quick appraisal of chord-progressions, without which fluent work is inconceivable, a sort of abbreviated reckoning is employed to indicate the value of a progression and to show its direction (about which the harmonic fluctuation gives us no information). For this purpose, we make use of the roots of the chords, and in our study of this subject we shall restrict ourselves to the simplest relations: those between the roots of two adjacent chords. These two roots, once they have been extracted from their chords, we shall now consider apart from the tonal masses in which they originated, simply as two tones of given pitches without chordal relations. As such, they form an interval which has all the char-

[121]

acteristics we observed in Chapter III. Here, as in that chapter, a
third is a strongly harmonic interval, while a second is essentially
melodic; in short, we stand once again before the whole series of
interval-values. This juxtaposition of roots derived from chords
is a reliable means of judging the value of a chord-progression,
equally useful for the analysis of progressions already in existence
and for the construction of new ones.

Let us examine the chord-progressions within Group A, which
because of their independence and complete certainty will furnish
the clearest illustrations of what has been said. The simplest progressions are those involving only the chords of sub-group I. In the
following example we see the roots of two adjacent chords first at
the distance of a fifth, then of a fourth, and so on up to the major
seventh (minor second).

A progression based on the interval of a fifth between its roots
naturally has a surer foundation than one based on a minor sixth:
this is the strongest of all chord-progressions. If we keep the values
of the chords equal (as we have determined to do here, confining
ourselves to the chords of group I), then the next best progression
after that based on a fifth is that based on a fourth. Then follow
in the familiar order progressions based on root-progressions of
a third and a sixth, in which the softness of the root-progression is
not only repeated but multiplied in the movement of the tonal
masses of the chords. The melodic step of a second is similarly
confirmed in the chord-progression based on it. The experience we

have had with Series 2 teaches us that a chord-progression based on a root-progression of a tritone will be the least valuable of all.

The nature of root-calculation should already be clear from the few examples given. It serves the same purpose in the realm of tones, roughly speaking, as logarithms do in the realm of numbers: the reckoning is done with small exponents, which represent the quantities sought. The accumulation of melodic steps in the chord-progressions, the product of multiplied melodic tensions, can be reduced to the harmless addition and subtraction of single tones. But apart from the fact that our tonal materials are numerically limited, reckoning with roots has one disadvantage as compared with that with logarithms: chords, which are the sums of the tones of which they are composed, are not definite quantities, for over the same root a great variety of chord structures is possible. Here an investigation of the two-voice framework and the harmonic fluctuation will clear up all ambiguity.

The ever-obtrusive tritone is not satisfied with affecting the individual chord, or with its influence upon chord-roots: it also has a bearing upon the tonal sums that are juxtaposed in chord-progressions. Progressions like the following

and similar ones always retain, despite the smoothest voice-leading, a certain unwieldiness, because the tritone is wedged in between them. That explains why the familiar progression of the tonic and dominant triads is satisfying when the dominant is a major triad, whereas when a minor triad on the dominant is connected with a major tonic the progression is less smooth on account of the tritone between the thirds of the two triads.

[123]

In the progressions from a minor tonic to a major dominant and from a minor tonic to a minor dominant (of course we are speaking only of progressions involving chords of group I), there is no tritone.

The strict antithesis of the unwieldy progressions obstructed by the tritone wedge is that in which all the tones move in minor seconds. This chromatic voice-leading produces the smoothest and most flowing progressions; it acts like a magic formula to make every imaginable chord-progression usable. The simultaneous movement of all voices over the same distance, though in different directions, brings the melodic step of the minor second so strongly into the foreground that the ear relegates the harmonic activity indicated by the root-progression to the background. This kind of universal joint cannot be used everywhere, on account of its soft and sliding effect, and it is particularly inappropriate in a style which in general makes very sparing use of chromaticism. Furthermore, its spell is weakened the moment the chromatic movement is not shared by all the voices. Yet even when only some of the voices move by half-tone steps, the chromatic influence is so strong that progressions which would otherwise be difficult to handle, on account of the position and context of the chords, may be made smooth by this means. This explains why in Figure 81 Examples b and d are smoother than the others: each contains two half-steps. In these progressions, the conspicuousness of the tritone is diminished by the chromatic voice-leading. Thus we experience once again in the realm of the simplest chord-relations what we observed in Figure 78, where the lack of root-progression was compensated for by the clearly defined harmonic fluctuation: the various forces at work in harmony may be so played off against one another that the sharpness of one element is made up for by the smoothness of another, and the weaknesses of one by the extra strength of another.

In the well-rounded progressions among chords of group I, lacking in tension as they are, such compensations for one force by another will take place only to a limited extent. But they become extremely significant when we introduce the sharper sounds of group III. The strong tendencies of the latter, arising from the fact of their containing numerous seconds or sevenths, require more careful treatment. Since it is not always appropriate to let these chords work themselves out in undiminished sharpness of sound, they can be adapted to their environment by means of smooth voice-leading, by gradualness of harmonic fluctuation, and by a smooth two-voice framework.

In reckoning roots, it makes no difference which octave they occur in. The differences in their position are of course of decisive importance to the harmonic fluctuation, but for the reckoning of roots a rough procedure suffices: we transpose all the roots, so far as possible, into the same octave, so that the intervals between them are always small.

With an understanding of root-calculation, harmonic fluctuation, and the two-voice framework, all chord-progressions using the materials of groups I and III can be easily handled. Formations which have always been very refractory, and the successful use of which has always been possible only by a constant process of trial and error, or by simple arbitrary decision, may now be handled with complete knowledge; they offer no more resistance to treatment than their more tractable comrades of group I.

A progression of which one member belongs to group I or III and the other to group V offers certain difficulties, because of the fact that the chord belonging to group V has no root. Since any one of its three tones may act as root representative, we may choose which one we wish to connect with the root of the other chord. In general, that one will be chosen which is the best connected to the roots of the chords preceding and following it. This procedure seems to smack of arbitrariness, but when we come to the analysis of more extended progressions we shall see that this is an illusion. The impression of arbitrary procedure will be heightened when we treat progressions involving two or more chords of group V. For in a progression of one of these chords to another, one has one's choice among six possible root representatives, and thus one can arrange the root-progression as one pleases. But in a wider view the number of possibilities becomes much smaller, so that the one best suited to our scale of values and to the goal of the progressions is easily to be found. The advantage of these chords—their ambiguity—is fully preserved in this treatment, for they contain in their very texture an indefinite, opalescent quality; yet they can no longer escape being drawn into an órderly sequence. We shall handle them with care, and define them at least sufficiently to make them fit the mould which their context of definite chords leaves open to them.

5

Progressions Involving Tritone Chords

The addition of chords from Group B raises the number of possibilities of progression enormously. When the independent chords of Group A are connected with chords of Group B, the tritone, which seeks resolution, and which gives the chords of Group B their character, sets up fields of force to which the chords of Group A offer more or less resistance according to their individual natures. Whenever a tritone chord is followed by a chord of Group A, the tritone is thereby resolved, and the pure sounds of group I, lending themselves willingly to this attraction, produce a feeling of complete relaxation after tension. Chords of group III following a tritone chord also resolve the tritone, it is true, but because of their own considerable tension (though they are free of tritones) the resolution they offer is not complete. Similarly, the progression of a tritone chord to a chord of group V may be only partially satisfactory, because where tension leaves, uncertainty enters. Progressions in the opposite direction—from a chord of Group A to a tritone chord—whip up the sound from rest to tension, and the more complicated the second chord, the greater the feeling of tension.

To gain a clear picture of the nature and value of all these progressions, let us compare the roots of the two chords in each case, as we have done in the progressions of Group A chords already discussed, and thus obtain a reduced and easily grasped image of the harmonic change. The resolution of the tritone, which we must also examine if we are to investigate the progression thoroughly, makes it necessary for us to add to our calculation. For this purpose we shall employ the guide-tone previously mentioned. In all progressions of a chord of Group B to a chord of Group A, the guide-tone of the B chord must move by a good interval to the root of the A chord if the resolution is to be satisfactory. The simplest resolutions occur when this takes place by the step of a second, or when the guide-tone remains stationary, being identical with the root of the A chord. In the second case, the difference in tension between the two chords can be but slight, since the holding over of an important factor cannot be more impressive than its motion by the step of a second. The reckoning of the guide-tone does not stamp any progressions as unusable, any more than did our other means of investigation based on the differing values of the intervals. Progressions of tritone chords in which the guide-tone proceeds by a good interval (the definitions of "good" and "bad" being derived from Series 2) to the root of the chord of resolution have, then, an advantage over those in which it proceeds by a less good interval. And this fact will enable the composer, in handling these often clumsy chords, to place exactly the right chord at the right place for his purposes.

The following examples show the application of the guide-tone principle:

Figure 83 shows progressions of chords of group II to chords of group I, the enharmonic identification of various guide-tones and roots in Examples d, f, and g, should, after what has been said, meet with objection only from those who are fanatics for correct writing. All these simple progressions may be produced without calculation of the guide-tone, simply with the help of the root-progressions. In the following examples (progressions of chords of group II to chords of group III) we could not make any accurate judgement of the value of the progressions without a conscious understanding of the treatment of the guide-tone.

In c and d of Figure 84, the roots progress by tritones. Now, when one tries these progressions out one will observe that c sounds quite satisfying, while d is less convincing. This is because the voice-leading in c is chromatic throughout, the resultant smoothness being emphasized by the holding through of the tone b^1, while the whole-tone step and the skip in d lay bare the tritone in the root-progression.

In Figure 85 tritone chords of group II are connected with the indeterminate chords of group V. The assumption of different root representatives makes possible in each case three different interpretations of the guide-tone progression.

More complicated progressions, in which the first chord is one of
group IV, are shown in Figures 86–88 (IV–I in 86, IV–III in 87,
IV–V in 88). The progressions using the indeterminate chords of
group V permit, as always, a choice of root representatives. In 88a,
the root-progression f♯-e avoids the tritone skip f♯-c, although the
tritone is still present in the progression of the guide-tone (a♯-e).
The root-progression f♯-g♯ yields a good progression of the guide-
tone, too, and is accordingly the best. It is almost impossible to
judge the connection of the very sharp chords of group IV with
those of group V—the augmented triad and the chord in fourths—
without reference to any other chords preceding or following. The
value of such progressions can be judged only from the wider harmonic context.

When several chords of Group B follow one another without
interruption, the tritone remains unresolved. Instead of a resolution,
each chord presents a new tritone. which keeps the harmony in
approximately equal, though perhaps differently focused, tension.
The succession of tension and relaxation which is indispensable
to musical structure may be produced in such progressions by the
harmonic fluctuation or by family relations among the chords. Not
until the entrance of a chord of Group A is the tritone resolved as
above described. Successions of chords within Group B are treated,
so far as the roots are concerned, like the chord-progressions already
discussed. The guide-tone of the tritone in the first chord moves
to the guide-tone of the second. The interval traversed in this suc-

cession is again the measure of the value of the progression (in terms of the known interval-values), although only secondarily so, since in such progressions the root-succession is of primary importance. Although the interval of the root-succession and the interval of the guide-tone succession should have values appropriate to the expressive value of the chord-progression itself, the two successions are dependent on each other only in relation to the two-voice harmonic interval based upon each separate root. The two lines of the root-progression and the guide-tone progression need not combine to make correct two-part writing. If each of the lines is logical in itself, and if at each point in their joint progression they form a clear and intelligible harmonic interval, it makes no difference whether they obey the rules of two-part writing or form the crudest infractions of those rules. Not until the resolution into a chord of Group A must the balance be restored by the progression of both root and guide-tone to the root of the chord of resolution.

The chords of group II and many of those of group IV have one particular characteristic. In a succession of two such tritone chords of which the roots in turn are separated by the distance of a tritone, there is a tritone also between the guide-tones of the two chords, and the tritone included in the first chord is also contained in the second:

This chain of tritones links these two chords so closely together that they seem almost like fractional parts of the same chord; they

[130]

thus perform good service when a close but highly tensed progression is needed, but they are quite out of place when a strong root-progression is desired.

Progressions within groups II or IV, or those from II to IV are thus easy to appraise:

If the progression is from a chord of group II or group IV to one of group VI, the root of the first chord moves to the most convenient tone of the indeterminate VI chord, as it does in the progressions from chords of Group A to those of group VI, already discussed.

The guide-tone of the first chord, too, goes to any convenient tone of the indeterminate chord, whether it is the same one to which the root proceeds or not. Here, too, it is only in a progression of two chords torn from its context that the choice is completely free. If the chord of group VI is between two other chords, the latter do not leave many possibilities open—whether because the guide-tones of the preceding and following chords require a particular tone between them, or because the following chord is one of Group A, of which the root is a common goal for both the guide-tone and the root of the preceding chord, and must be reached in the smoothest possible way from the last definite guide-tone over the assumed guide-tone as a bridge. In progressions within group VI, the calculation of the root representatives suffices.

6

Family Relationship

The Construction of Tonal Spheres

One last force that operates in chord-progressions remains to be investigated: harmonic family-relationship. Here, too, we may make use of the abbreviated reckoning that served us so well in considering movement in chord-connection: we shall extract the roots of the chords, and work with them instead of with the complete chords.

When one hears the three tones c-e-g sung or played in succession, each tone being of equal duration

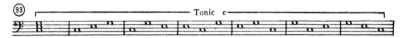

the ear perceives them as a broken c-major triad. It always takes c as the root and the other two tones as satellites of c. Even when the three tones appear in different order, c is always taken as the most important, and we know why this is true. According to the interval-values of Series 2, the fifth c-g outlined by the three tones is stronger than either of the thirds c-e or e-g, and since c is the root of the fifth it dominates the entire group and becomes the center of a tonal sphere consisting of these three tones: it is their *tonic*. If three successive root-tones form a broken chord of groups I or II, the root of this chord is the tonic of the succession:

Tonic: a   f   a♭   c

To be sure, this relation can be so affected by rhythmic considerations that some tone other than the one determined purely by the interval-values may, by emphasis of metric position or duration, become the tonic. This is true even in melodic successions of individual tones which bear no chord-structures, and which because of their primarily linear significance offer a certain resistance to the influence of time-values. Of course, in so strongly chordal a succession as c-e-g, even the sharpest melodic emphasis, the greatest stress, and the longest duration of the e or the g will not deprive the c of its primary importance. But in melodic successions of less strongly harmonic design, such as c-f-e for example, duration and position in the measure are of decisive importance in determining the tonic: the stressed portion of the measure, the longest note, or the final note is needed to tell us which is the principal tone of the group. When chords are built on these tones as roots, the weight of the tonal masses makes the interval-relationships of the roots even less free; they are affected even more easily by stress and duration than in the case of successions of single tones, and their independence is accordingly still smaller. Another factor of importance in the determination of the tonic is the value of the various chords erected on the roots in question. A chord of group I will always try to act as a tonal center for chords of lower value, and thus may at times come into mild conflict with the harmonic values of the root-succession intervals. The skilful exploitation of all these forces produces even within the narrowest limits a richness of tonal possibilities.

A succession of roots forming a broken chord of groups III or IV is particularly susceptible to the influences of rhythm and of the harmonic fluctuation, since it does not have the stability of triad formations. If its tones are all of equal duration, and without special stress, the root of the best interval is again the tonic. The same is true of groupings which, because of their strongly melodic character, can hardly be perceived as forming chords. Root-successions which form a chord of groups V or VI are almost always so affected by rhythmic considerations and by the harmonic fluctuation that their uncertainty is dispelled.

Since according to our chord-table any group of tones may be considered as a chord, whereas in the succession of roots obviously not every possible chord of groups III or IV is taken by the ear as a broken chord, no precise line can be drawn between root-successions which count as chords and those which do not. In general, the feeling that successive roots form a broken chord does not

[133]

go far beyond the triad. Slight additions like neighboring tones and passing tones are counted as auxiliary to triad-formations, while the more complicated root-successions are split up into sections which, owing to the thirds and fifths they contain, show the triad-like formations which are lacking in the group taken as a whole.

A succession of chords of Group A must consist of at least three chords if it is to represent a tonal entity. A succession of only two roots does not clearly reveal any tonal coherence, for the interval formed by two adjacent roots has its own root, which to a superficial glance might seem to be the center of the group. But the mass of tones contained in the chords require a more definite determination; they are not satisfied with the confirmation of the central tone by only one other tone. That is why the juxtaposition of two other tones, supporting the central tone on both sides, is necessary to place that tone definitely.

A prominent position among the chords of a group is always held by their goal, the final chord (see the next section, p. 138, on the cadence). This chord, representing the end of a harmonic path, claims such a large share of the hearer's attention that it may always be regarded as one of the most important chords of the group, even when its structure and the position of its root in the tonal sphere are not of the highest value. If it belongs to the same group as the preceding chords, its position at the end of the group makes it play the leading rôle. If it belongs to a group of lower rank, and accordingly does not quite succeed in achieving that rôle, it nevertheless has such importance that a tonality otherwise stable enough may be undermined by it. As far as the root-successions are concerned, this means that the normal interval-values are modified somewhat in favor of the last tone of each such succession. Here again, inverted intervals, weaker than uninverted, offer less resistance.

Tonal Center: d   d   c   c

In root-successions like the foregoing, the preponderant significance of the final tone robs the earlier tones of so much value that in the

[134]

first two examples of Figure 94ᵃ the f, which should really have the principal rôle, as root of a fourth, yields to the d. Similarly the a of the last two examples yields to the c: the root of the interval which is in itself higher in value (fourth, minor sixth) cannot hold its own against the power of the final tone.

The situation is different where chords of Group B are concerned. Several such chords are not needed to produce a feeling of tonality; a single one is enough. The tritone contained in them forces the ear to assume a chord of resolution. Although the ear does this willingly enough, it does not know in which direction to resolve the tritone. Thus the sounding of a single tritone chord is enough to create a feeling of tonality, but the tonal center is not defined. Only when the tritone is resolved can one know which chord-root is the tonal center:

Tonal Center: c   f♯   d♯

When a chord of Group B is followed by a chord of Group A, the root of the latter is the tonal center. It follows that in a series of successive tritone chords the tonality cannot be determined until the chord of resolution. When there is no chord of resolution the tonal center may be deduced from the roots just as it would be in a series of chords of Group A:

Tonal Center: g♯

The uninterrupted tritone tension dulls the hearer's senses to the point where they cease to notice it, and fail to feel the need of resolution, as long as resolution is completely avoided. In such a case the best interval between the roots of the chords serves to determine the tonal center, which is the root of this interval unless the final tone lays claim to that position.

If we are dealing exclusively with chords from group II, the tonal

[135]

center is not very stable, for the dominant effect of the tritone does not permit the tone which would result from our reckoning to be completely satisfying as the tonal center.

Dominant: E
Tonic: A

In such cases this tone too is of dominant effect, and thus we may say that in an unresolved series of chords of group II the tonal center is to be regarded as the dominant of a tonic lying below it. This implied tonic is a fifth below the dominant because the un-resolved tritone of the final chord would resolve most naturally into an interval whose root would be a fifth below the root of the tritone chord.

Successions of chords belonging to group IV do not need this special consideration. If a series of them occurs without a chord of resolution, the assumption of a tonic lying below their roots is un-necessary. Chords of groups V and VI are treated, once their root has been determined, just like chords of Groups A or B with defi-nite roots; in a long, uninterrupted succession of these chords (which in practice will hardly occur) the tonic could not be de-termined, and the tonal relationship of the succession would remain indefinite.

How many chords are needed to produce a tonal center?

How is the Tonic found?

A Chords without Tritones | **B** Chords containing Tritones

I

3 Chords

TONIC:

Principal tone of
the group formed
by the chord-roots

2 Chords
TONIC: Root of the
chord of resolution

II

2 Chords
The last of a group
of chord-roots is
the Dominant of a
TONIC lying a
fifth lower

3 Chords
TONIC:
Same as in I

2 Chords: TONIC: Root of
the chord of resolution

2 Chords: TONIC: Root of
chord of resolution

2 Chords
TONIC:
Same as in II

III

IV

3 Chords

TONIC:

Same as in I

2 Chords
TONIC: Root of the
chord of resolution

2 Chords

TONIC:

Same as in I

V After determination of the root, to
be treated the same as I

VI After determination of the root, to
be treated the same as II

TONIC:
Indeterminate

TONIC:
Indeterminate

The plan of this table corresponds to that of the main table at the end of this volume. Double rectangles
enclose progressions within one sub-group. Arrows indicate progressions from one sub-group to another.

[137]

7

The Cadence

The type of tonal connection which has been described is so concentrated, owing both to its almost purely harmonic content and to its brevity, that it appears in actual music only under certain conditions. One usually feels that a design is well planned and well executed only when a brief and concentrated root-succession of this sort has rich melodic decoration, or when other harmonic ingredients space out and smooth over the abruptness of such unerring and unhindered movement straight to a goal. But there is one place where the strongest and most concentrated chord-successions of this kind perform an admirable service: in the cadence. Cadences are chord-progressions of which the effect·is strongly final, and which in many styles are actual *formulae of conclusion,* composed, like all chord-successions, of rhythmic, melodic, and harmonic elements, but in which the tendency to bring a development to a provisional or complete ending is all-powerful. In them, the rhythm confines itself to a few clear and unmistakable time-divisions, the melodic steps proceed directly to their goals, the two-voice framework employs the simplest intervals, and the harmonic fluctuation exhibits the most unambiguous progression from less satisfactory to more satisfactory chords, from tension to relaxation. Their root-successions cannot produce anything different from what is contained in any other chord-progressions, but the predominatingly structural purpose of the cadence results in an intensification of the root-relations. Thus the increased value of the final chord of a succession, mentioned in the previous section, is even more important in the cadence than in other chord-successions, for every factor that contributes to the final effect of the cadence is grist to its mill. Even in root-successions which would ordinarily be indeterminate (such as a broken tritone) or in which more than one tonal center would have to be assumed (as in broken chords of groups V or VI), the final tone in the cadence is so strong that it becomes the tonal center. The extent to which every element in the cadence subordinates itself to the structural drive towards

[138]

finality is shown by the fact that in the chords making up a cadence even the highest laws of clean writing are often disobeyed, and consecutive parallels, both open and covered, ugly melodic leaps, chromatic slides, and other devices which would ordinarily be used only with the greatest reserve and only for particular expressive effects, are employed without hesitation.

A cadence, like any other succession which is to determine a tonal center, requires three chords of Group A, or only two chords if the first is of Group B and the second of Group A. It is the participation of the individual forces, measured by methods now familiar, that determines the value of a cadence. Just as elsewhere, the root-succession presents a reduced picture of the harmonic progression. The strongest cadences are those in which the intervals of the root-succession are either exclusively fourths and fifths, or consist of a fourth or a fifth plus a step of a second:

The root-succession in which the tonal center is preceded by its fourth and its fifth forms the ideal cadence. What makes it ideal is not only the succession of closely related tones. For the chords built on the fourth and the fifth embody (at least when they are simple triads, the one on the fifth being major) a tritone divided between them, which is resolved in the final chord. To the strong relationship of the first and second roots to the third, which is strongly counterbalanced by their melodic relation to each other, there is added a sort of harmonic short-circuit between the first two chords in the shape of the oblique tritone between them, which contributes significantly to the tendency to a strong close.

This same tritone relation results from the cadential root-progres-

sion major second—fifth—tonic, and accordingly this progression is also very strong:

But it is not as strong as the first one, because it substitutes for the hard step of a second between the first two tones the more closely related skip of a fourth.

Cadential formations in which the final root is preceded by its fifth, but the fifth is preceded by some tone other than the fourth or the major second, vary in value according to the position of this new tone. We are here obviously in borderland territory, where the forces of Series 1 and Series 2 now conflict and now coincide. Take for example a chord-succession of which the roots are a-g-c:

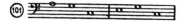

In terms of Series 2 we have first a second and then a fifth; the fifth, being the better interval, determines the tonal center, which is c. According to the values of Series 2, the root-succession e-g-c would produce a better chord-progression, for the third e-g is higher in value than the second a-g. In isolated progressions of two chords, this is true, but in a cadence it is not just the relations between each two adjacent chords that count, for the ear relates them to the tonal center of the group, which is easily determined according to the interval-values of this same Series 2. Now, in the question of relations to a central tone it is Series 1 that governs, as has been suggested earlier. Although we shall comprehend the full importance of this principle only in the construction of extended chord-successions, yet the organizing power of Series 1 is clearly to be observed even in these cadential groups of only three chords. In the root-succession a-g-c, the a is closer to the tonal center c (as we know from Series 1) than the e in the succession e-g-c; accordingly, the cadential progression built on the root-succession a-g-c̣ is the stronger. There follow in order the progressions built on e-g-c, e♭-g-c, and a♭-g-c. The progression d-g-c illustrates the coinciding of the pure interval-values and the relationship-values:

The d is not very closely related to the c and seems almost, by its melodic tendency, to act as a neighboring tone of c. At the same time, the high interval-value of the skip d-g gives the d so much force that it is hard to tell whether it is the interval-values of Series 2 or the relationships of Series 1 that are more active in this case. The root-successions b♭-g-c, b-g-c, and d♭-g-c, show a strong melodic cast in the seconds b♭-c, b-c, and d♭-c, interrupted by the strong fifth g-c; the harmonic power of cadences built upon these successions is accordingly much lower. In the root-succession f♯-g-c

the tritone f♯-c does not fully count, since the f♯ is taken merely as the neighboring tone of the g.

If the tonal center of a cadential group of chords is reached by skip of a fourth downwards,

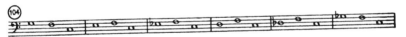

the value of the cadence is diminished, in accordance with both the interval-values of Series 2 and the relationships of Series 1. The great firmness of the cadences in which the final interval is a fifth is here changed into something smoother, but also something strange and inaccessible. And here, too, the quality of the cadence diminishes with the decreasing relation of the tone before the last interval to the tonal center.

A skip of a third between the tonal center and the root preceding it

makes the cadence soft and amiable; while a major second at the same place

shows, in accordance with its melodic character, the familiar harmonic sharpness, which cannot be made up for, even by placing a better interval before it. The use of the minor second (upwards or downwards) just before the tonal center

results, owing to its leading-tone tendency, in the mildest of all cadences. The tritone produces the poorest cadence, and can be used only with considerable help from other factors—rhythmic, melodic, and even dynamic and expressive.

The briefer cadences, consisting only of a chord of Group B followed by its resolution in a chord of Group A, may be appraised according to the same precepts. When there are only two roots, it is hard to recognize the fact that they represent not only an interval-value of Series 2 but also a relationship of Series 1; but in a larger harmonic context, without which a cadence-formation would have no purpose, these cadences take their place without hesitation.

8

Larger Harmonic Relations

Degree-Progression

Root-calculation permits us to form a judgement about the succession of two chords, and enables us to recognize without difficulty the tonal relations which underlie cadences. Roots are our guide, too, through larger harmonic sections, in which they are the supports of a wide tonal structure of which the thrusts and tensions act in accordance with the family-relationships of Series 1. This series of tonal values is here the undisputed master. The roots which support the burdens of larger harmonic groupings may be called *degrees,* and their succession in accordance with the demands of Series 1 the *degree-progression.*

According to a view widely held, larger harmonic developments are simply extended cadences. This is inaccurate insofar as it ignores the fact that, as we have seen, the structural tendency towards an ending in a cadence subordinates all other factors to it, while in other harmonic developments what is sought is the free unfolding of rhythm, melody, and harmony. But one thing such free developments do have in common with cadences: the roots of their chords must exhibit tonal coherence if the chord-successions which take place above them are to be understandable.

In a succession of only three roots, it was not difficult to determine the tonal center with the help of the interval-values. But when the degree-progression consists of more than three tones, the expanding force of the tonal relationships robs the interval-values of some of their significance. In such cases, the tone which attracts attention by recurring most often is usually to be taken as the tonal center; only in very short degree-progressions, in which no tone is repeated, do the interval-values still reign. But it is best to confirm the determination of the tonal center by subsequent repetition in any case; otherwise the ear may, in its quest for the tonal center, seize upon some tone other than that which is intended by the composer.

We can, however, spare the ear both the quest and the mistake. Besides the repetition of a root, it is the surrounding tones that determine the tonal center, according to their relationship to it. The closest relationships are its best supports. If the tonal center is to possess particular stability, one had better see to it that there is a nice balance of intervals in the degree-progression centering around it. If only the closest relatives are called upon, then it is best to use the fourth as a counterpoise to the fifth. For the further development of the degree-progression it is advantageous to use a balanced variety of tones of close and distant relationship, containing among them as many good intervals—fifths and fourths—as possible. Samples of such arrangements, which may undergo the most varied changes, are contained in the following examples:

The degree-progression gives us a means of combating the effects of harmonic fluctuation in chord-successions. If the chords have very varied harmonic weight, being members of very unequal groups, the degree-progression may be very smooth, consisting largely of third-relationships and leading tones. If, on the other hand, the chords all belong to the same or closely related groups, and so vary little or not at all in tension, then the degree-progression must introduce variety, arranging contrasts between light and heavy, strong and weak, among the graded family-relationships of its tones.

The guide-tones of the tritone chords have no effect on the degree-progression. They are not continuously present, and disappear altogether when several chords of Group A follow one another; they appear only from time to time when occasional tritone chords are interpolated, and compose a continuous series only when a number of chords of Group B follow one another uninterruptedly.

The succession of guide-tones which results in this latter case is quite independent of the degree-progression of the roots, as we saw when we considered the connection of chords of Group B. But between the extreme points of such a succession (which are always at places where a chord of Group A causes the line of the roots to coincide with that of the guide-tones) the melodic development must be, like the degree-progression, logically developed and based on the relationship-values of Series 1. Unlike the degree-progression, however, the guide-tone line does not need to rest on a single tonal center, and in particular not upon that of the degree-progression.

[144]

An ill-designed degree-progression can prevent the free unfolding of the chords above it. Therefore in constructing the degree-progression anything that would obstruct the free unfolding of the harmony is to be avoided. Here, as everywhere in the realm of artistic work, no unfailing rule and no prohibition valid without exceptions can be given for the construction of good designs. What is good in one place may be of lamentable effect in another. Nevertheless, for the degree-progression which is not too strongly influenced by the expressive requirements of the composition, or too clearly articulated into sections by cadence-formations, sequences, or other groupings, a few principles may be formulated. The observance of these principles, when the two-voice framework and the harmonic fluctuation are skilfully handled, will insure a smooth series of chord-progressions.

In a normal degree-progression the following factors are *detrimental* to the effect:

1. The absence over a long period of the strong-relationship intervals of the fourth and fifth:

This brings the danger that the less closely related intervals may subject themselves to the organizing force of Series 2 and thus determine a new tonal center, different from that of the degree-progression.

2. The melodic interval of the tritone. It can be used with good effect only where one of its tones becomes the upper or lower neighbor of a better interval, or when the expression of a composition calls for closely connected but not strong harmonic progressions.

[145]

If for one reason or another it is desired to maintain the effect of the tritone intact in the degree-progression, but without its being too prominent, the insertion of a rhythmically unimportant neighboring tone (of course bearing a chord upon it) to either the upper or the lower tone of the tritone will make the progression somewhat more flowing. The disturbing awkwardness that characterizes most progressions' based on a tritone in the degree-progression can be overcome, as we have seen, by chromatic voice-leading in some or all of the parts.

3. Broken chords of any easily recognized species except major and minor triads.

Even the thirds of triads bind the chords built upon these roots very closely together. If the degree-progression traverses the tones of an augmented triad, the uncertainty of that chord is transferred to the progression. Degree-progressions in the shape of a tritone chord almost always produce, because of the strong power of association of the tritone, unsatisfactory chord-progressions. Broken-chord formations of whatever nature, even those consisting of as many as four different tones, must be handled with especial care if they are to produce a satisfactory effect.

4. Chromatic progressions—that is, several minor seconds in uninterrupted succession, or so little separated that the feeling of chromaticism persists:

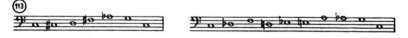

5. Explicitly melodic treatment—that is, serious impairment of the clarity and intelligibility of the succession by the presence of subordinate tones: passing tones, anticipations, etc.;

The reason for all these rules is the multiplication of all the virtues and defects of the degree-progression in the chord-progressions which take place above it. The skip of a tritone, which in a single melodic line is less good than other intervals but cannot do too much harm, naturally brings about unpleasant consequences when it draws a considerable number of tones lying above it into its orbit. And the splitting up of the line of the degree-progression into very small subordinate parts, which are understandable only as parts of a larger whole, must lead to complete incomprehensibility when it is magnified by being projected into the chord-successions. Yet none of these rules absolutely forbids anything. If the particular expression of a passage demands a tritone progression, the composer must use it; if chromaticism in the degree-progression is the means that will most clearly express the sense of a passage, it will be used without hesitation. The rules here given are warnings only. They are intended to help the composer avoid the unintentional use of harmonic procedures which will stand in the way of the complete realization of his intentions.

As with the two-voice framework, in the normal degree-progression organ-points do not count. In organ-point formations, the degree-progression needs to take the tone of the organ-point into account only at the main points of harmonic support, where the stationary bass-tone forms with the tones above it the simplest and clearest chords, or chords in which a very closely related tone occurs. In the chords between these points, the organ-point in the bass is left out of the reckoning, and the chords above it follow their own, independent degree-progression. The same is true of organ-points in middle or upper voices: the stationary tone can be left out of the reckoning.

In successions of identical intervals or chords moving in parallel motion, involving some or all of the voices—successions of fifths, sixth-chords, *etc.*—the reckoning may be simplified by taking only the more important points in the succession into account, provided that the tempo is not so slow as to give each of the intervals or chords its own harmonic value.

9

Modulation

We see in the tonal arrangement of the degree-progression how —despite the greatest strictness in the choice of material and in the construction of the harmony out of the interplay of elemental rhythmic, melodic, and harmonic forces—the boundaries of tonality have been extended. We have stepped from a small realm dominated by three triads and fenced in by modal scales to a broad land full of chords of all designs and governed by tonal relations. We must think back, disregarding historical considerations, to what was needed to accommodate a D♭ major triad in the key of C major, in order to realize what a narrow world we have left behind us: the minor triad had to be transformed in the imagination to a major one, and two tones had to be accommodated which did not occur in the triad proper to the key:

The form in which the chord really appeared flatly contradicted the analytical procedure that had to be applied to it. Is it not clearer and simpler to regard such a chord (the Neapolitan triad) as a chord of sub-group I with the relationship-value derived from its progenitor tone and measured according to Series 1? Let us remember, too, how arbitrarily all chords not built up in thirds had to be explained. Now we can determine their place in harmonic procedure just as easily and definitely as that of the triads. But although we can now embrace all conceivable chords within a tonality, and arrange them according to Series 1, we must burst the bonds of a single tonality. Every tone seeks an importance greater than that which it has simply as a tone, or as a descendant of a progenitor tone, or as a part of a chord; it seeks to become the fundamental of an overtone series, the progenitor of a new Series 1

[148]

of its own, the tonal center of a degree-progression. When we yield to this tendency, when we allow one tone to usurp the place of another as tonal center of a degree-progression, we are modulating.

Modulation as an end in itself, isolated from the logical development of all the elements of musical writing, is an absurdity, no more possible than a chord-progression free of all but harmonic influences, or a melody in which melodic force alone operates. Yet in order to understand the nature of modulation we must separate it from its context and study it alone, just as we did with harmonic fluctuation, or the two-voice framework. Root-calculation, which has shortened our labors in other fields, does so here, too. We can determine the presence of modulation from the construction of the degree-progression alone; consideration of the progressions from root to root will show us the nature and the value of a modulation.

The prerequisite of a modulation is a firmly established tonal center as a point of departure. A tonality which is not definitely settled will not do, for it does not offer enough resistance to the subsequent tonal center, and accordingly becomes subservient to it. A tonal sphere is set up in the manner familiar to us, by the grouping of chord-tones around a tonal center. The new tonal sphere will be set up in the same way, through the grouping of roots around a new center. Since one tonality can include every kind of chord, it is not always easy to find the exact location of the boundary separating the two tonal domains. But we owe to the phenomenon of tonal relations the fact that we are able at all to feel our way among the degree-progression tones with their chords, belonging to the most varied tonal centers, and determine to which one each belongs. Within a single degree-progression, we always hear as the center of a tonal sphere that tone which occurs repeatedly within a limited space of time, or that one which outranks the others by virtue of its position at the end of a cadence, or finally that one which is supported by the presence of the tones most closely related to it (the fifth and the fourth). Yet the continual movement of a degree-progression in fifths and fourths does not necessarily produce a continual changing of tonality. Since the root-successions of a degree-progression are to be brought as close together as possible by means of octave transpositions, many of the tones to which the degree-progression moves by fifths can be brought into close proximity with the tonal center, where—as the third or the second of the latter, say—they are outshone by its fourths and fifths. It is true, as we have previously stated, that the clear significance of a degree-progression can be disturbed by an abundance of chords above it belonging to groups III and IV. The degree-progression and the fluctuation may actually conflict. In such cases the triads are what help us to an understanding of the harmonic development. Just as the ear in hearing intervals seeks for the natural ratios, and tries to hear the clouded intervals as pure ones, so among chords the triad is the ear's natural unit of measure, which it tries to recognize wherever it can, and which it uses to help it in forming a judgement of other chords. In the ebb and flow of the most awkward chord-successions, triads will always stick out as points of rest, and will help, along with the tonal centers established by the degree-progression, to support the tonality—except where the composer wishes to leave the listener in doubt about the tonality for a brief period, and therefore uses a fair number of obscure chords.

The gradation of chord-weights enables us to set up chord-progressions in which two tonalities are at one point juxtaposed in the sharpest contrast and without connection. In the degree-progression this is not possible, because even those tones which have the most distant relationship to a tonal center are yet not completely unrelated to it. If these tones are skilfully worked into the degree-progression, the tonality will be supported by the tones standing in the best relationship to its tonal center, and we shall not need to assume constant changes of tonality in order to explain the presence of groupings only distantly related. Within the domain of new tonal centers the relationships to the old one are of course no longer valid, for the original Series 1 has been replaced by new ones, belonging to new tonal centers.

Between the parts of a degree-progression which are closely tied by skips of fourths and fifths to their respective centers, there are always passages that may belong to either sphere, passages where the tonalities overlap:

or there are transitional tonalities which link the others. In such cases, the ear has time to loosen its hold on the old tonal center, and to accustom itself to the new one before yielding completely to it. The clearer the way leading from one tonal center to the next, the more satisfactory the modulation. In such arrangements, the transitional sections of the degree-progression are so arranged that their function is obvious. They are subordinate and complementary to the tonal groupings which stand out as the bearers of tonality.

Often it is impossible to draw clear boundaries for either the principal or the subordinate tonal groupings; one listener hears the change as occurring at one place, another at another. But this is not a shortcoming; on the contrary, one of the greatest charms of modulation lies in the exploitation of this very uncertainty in the transitional passages.

The tonal centers of all the tonalities of a composition produce, when they are connected without the inclusion of any of the intervening tones, a second degree-progression, which should be constructed along the same lines as the first one, built of the roots of all the chords. Here we see the full unfolding of the organizing power of Series 1. The entire harmonic construction of a piece may be perceived in this way: against one tonal center chosen from among many roots others are juxtaposed which either support it or compete with it. Here, too, the tonal center that reappears most often, or that is particularly strongly supported by its fourth and its fifth, is the most important. As a tonal center of a higher order, it dominates a whole movement or a whole work. Exact statement of the principles of tonal organization is outside the bounds of theoretical discussion, and belongs rather to the teaching of composition itself. We shall therefore leave the subject after these few suggestions.

10

Atonality and Polytonality

Does not the discussion of tonality contained in the preceding section contradict what was promised in the Introductory section of Chapter I? What good is a new theory of composition if it leads straight back to the old, "worn-out" concept of tonality?

We have seen that tonal relations are founded in Nature, in the characteristics of sounding materials and of the ear, as well as in the pure relations of abstract numerical groups. We cannot escape the relationship of tones. Whenever two tones sound, either simultaneously or successively, they create a certain interval-value; whenever chords or intervals are connected, they enter into a more or less close relationship. And whenever the relationships of tones are played off one against another, tonal coherence appears. It is thus quite impossible to devise groups of tones without tonal coherence. Tonality is a natural force, like gravity. Indeed, when we consider that the root of a chord, because of its most favorable vibration-ratio to the other tones, and the lowest tone of a chord, because of the actually greater dimension and weight of its wave, have greater importance than the other tones, we recognize at once that it is gravitation itself that draws the tones towards their roots and towards the bass line, and that relates a multiplicity of chords to the strongest among them. If we omit from consideration the widely held notion that everything in which the ear and the understanding are not at once completely at home is atonal (a poor excuse for a lack of musical training and for following the path of least resistance), we may assert that there are but two kinds of music: good music, in which the tonal relations are handled intelligently and skilfully, and bad music, which disregards them and consequently mixes them in aimless fashion. There are many varieties between these two extremes, and of course it does not follow that all music in which the tonal relations are beautifully worked out is good music. But in all good music account is taken of them, and no music which disregards them can be satisfying, any more than could a building in which the most elementary laws of the vertical and horizontal disposition of masses were disregarded. For the creation of tonality it is all the same, being a matter of style and period, or of the manner in which a composer works, what kind of chord material is employed. A piece that consists primarily of very harsh and grating chords need not be atonal; and, on the other hand, limitation to the purest triads is no guarantee of clean tonal relationships.

The only music which can really be called atonal, therefore, is the work of a composer who is motivated perhaps by a consciousness of the inadequacy of old styles to the musical needs of our day, perhaps by a search for an idiom that will express his own feelings, perhaps by sheer perversity, to invent tonal combinations which do not obey the laws of the medium and cannot be tested by the simplest means of reckoning. Such a man is not impelled by the instinct of the musician, who even in what seems his blindest groping never loses the true path entirely from view. But even among the music which can be completely analyzed there are two types which, although they cannot be called atonal, yet by the accumulation of harmonic means of expression place too great a burden on the listening ear for it to be able to follow them completely. One of these types, although it starts from diatonic premises, works with the material of the chromatic scale, and packs in so closely a multitude of dominant relations, alterations, and enharmonic changes, that the key is bursting with harmonic groups of short duration. The ear may succumb to an excess of harmonic procedures each reasonable in itself. The other type, by a continuous use of chords of groups III and IV, produces an opaque kind of harmony which in its avoidance of any chord resembling a triad seems to fly in the face of Nature. Neither of these types can be made reasonable by the logic of its degree-progression; both are too crowded with material to be enjoyed. The development of music has left far behind the style of accumulated dominant relationships within short spaces of time, in favor of more important things. This style was developed by the German post-Wagnerian school. About 1900 it dominated the entire technique of composition, and it was still throwing up sizable waves as recently as the second decade of the present century, after which it quickly disappeared. The other style, which as a reaction to the outmoded diatonic style and the exaggerated technique of over-subtle harmonic relations and enharmonic changes, made great use of the sharpest chords, is still widely cultivated. We may assume that it will give way to a quieter and more enlightened style as soon as the quite praise-worthy joy of discovery on the part of composers and their pre-occupation with technical speculation become less important, and the accumulated knowledge of the expanded tonal materials and their laws prepares the way for a fuller and higher craft of composition.

There are today a considerable number of composers who issue works that they call atonal. To what extent the atonality of these compositions rests upon the lack of a convincing degree-progression and to what extent it is a more or less developed tonality concealed by an uninterrupted succession of sharp sonorities, the reader himself can determine by extracting the degree-progressions of such pieces. Doubtless these composers see in their freedom from tonality a liberty that will lift their art to the infinity of time and space. Apart from the fact that I consider it impossible to abolish the inherent characteristics of the medium, I do not believe that liberty is achieved by substituting mere variety for the principle of natural order. Nowhere does Nature give us any indication that it would be desirable to play off a certain number of tones against one an-other in a given duration and pitch-range. Arbitrarily conceived rules of that sort can be devised in quantities, and if styles of composition were to be based upon them, I can conceive of far more comprehensive and more interesting ones. To limit oneself to home-made tonal systems of this sort seems to me a more doctrinaire proceeding than to follow the strictest diatonic rules of the most dried-up old academic. Is it not strange that the same composers who worship harmonic freedom—or what they mistake for freedom, which is only a dead end which they have not yet recognized as such—have been taken in as, regards musical structure by a formalism that makes the artificialities of the early Netherland contrapuntists seem like child's play?

The existence of this style seems to me only to lend final confirmation to the fact, everywhere to be observed, of the disappearance of understanding judgement and critical sense in the field of music. But already a decline is noticeable in the interest manifested in this music based on rules dictated by fashion and contrary to nature.

Anyone to whom a tone is more than a note on paper or a key pressed down, anyone who has ever experienced the intervals in singing, especially with others, as manifestations of bodily tension, of the conquest of space, and of the consumption of energy, anyone who has ever tasted the delights of pure intonation by the continual displacement of the comma in string-quartet playing, must come to the conclusion that there can be no such thing as atonal music, in which the existence of tone-relationships is denied. The decline in the value placed upon tonality is based on the system of equal temperament, a compromise which is presented to us by the keyboard as an aid in mastering the tonal world, and then pretends to be that world itself. One needs only to have seen how the most fanatical lover of the piano will close his ears in horror at the falseness of the tempered chords of his instrument, once he has compared them a few times with those produced by a harmonium in pure intonation, to realize that with the blessing of equal temperament there entered into the world of music—lest the bliss of musical mortals be complete—a curse as well: the curse of too easy achievement of tone-connections. The tremendous growth of piano music in the last century is attributable to it, and in the "atonal" style I see its final fulfillment—the uncritical idolatry of tempered tuning.

The concept of atonality arose at the end of the first World War. At that time there appeared, among much other propaganda material, a periodical which proposed to examine "atonal and antitonal" formations. The difference between the two forms of nontonal music was never established, because no one could conceive of what was represented by "antitonality". So atonality was left, but no one ever established exactly what that concept represented either. Today we know that there can be no such thing as atonality, unless we are to apply that term to harmonic disorder. The vagueness of the conception, arising from its negative origin—here even

[155]

less fruitful than in other fields of creation—, caused it to grow from a technical term into a popular catchword, used by some to praise to the skies any music they did not understand, and by others to condemn whatever they did not like, whether it consisted of strange harmonies, muted trumpets, *fortissimo* outbursts, or new experiments in structure.

There is another catchword that dates from the post-War period: polytonality. The game of letting two or more tonalities run along side by side and so achieving new harmonic effects is, to be sure, very entertaining for the composer, but the listener cannot follow the separate tonalities, for he relates every simultaneous combination of sounds to a root—and thus we see the futility of the game. Every simultaneous combination of sounds must have one root, and only one; one cannot conceive of additional roots somewhere above, belonging to other tonal spheres. Even the craziest harmonic combinations can result in only one degree-progression. The ear judges the total sound, and does not ask with what intentions it was produced. Skilful planning of the harmonic fluctuation will eliminate all accidental effects such as always come about when tonal successions belonging to different tonal domains are capriciously combined. But since organic work, growing out of natural roots, will always stand on a firmer basis than the arbitrary combination of different elements, polytonality is not a practical principle of composition.

11

Practical Application

A true musician believes only in what he hears. No matter how ingenious a theory is, it means nothing to him until the evidence is placed before him in actual sound. For the reader who has not held back from the assertions previously made in this book, I will now give a practical example of the procedure which results from the combination of all the technical devices described. It will be seen that a task may thus be accomplished which could not be accomplished with other means, unless long training in playing and hearing had made our tonal sense an infallible guide. But experience tells us that in most musicians the sense of the value of complicated chords is not nearly developed enough to provide a source of unerring judgements. Even if in the imaginative process, in the sheer formation of the conceptions of musical phenomena, it performs invaluable services, it is insufficient as soon as one tries to note down the imagined sounds. Just as in the literature that is written in letters, so in that written in notes everything must be clear and completely analyzable to the person who knows how to read it. The true work of art does not need to wrap any veil of mystery about its external features. Indeed the very hallmark of great art is that only above and beyond the complete clarity of its technical procedure do we feel the essential mystery of its creative power. We must therefore be able to illuminate the darkest corners of a composition, and explain its construction completely. There are doubters who will not approve of such a procedure, because they are entangled in older theories, and perhaps also are angry and somewhat sad about what they call the coldness of feeling with which we strip bare matters which they would rather keep clothed in the semi-darkness of twilight. (In technical matters there can be no question of the temperature of our feelings; the true secrets begin, as we have said, on a much higher level.) But those of them who are not ill-willed in their disapproval must at least admit that new prospects are opened up for the technique of composition. Let anyone who, on the other hand, rejects our procedure out of mere antipathy try to arrive at more convincing conclusions by better means.

The conditions which I have set for myself in the treatment of the following example are far harder than one would ever find in actual music. I have purposely chosen so artificially complicated a case to show that even such problems can be solved. How much easier then must be the solution of the problems of free composition, which can never contain more than a small fraction of the difficulties of the following problem!

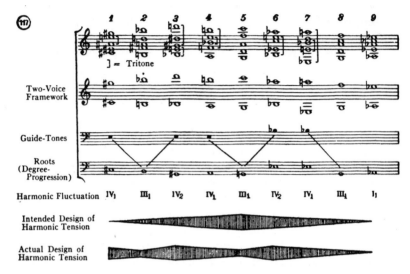

Suppose we were to find in a piece of music the foregoing series of chords. Let us grant that it sounds horrible—but can you honestly say that you have never encountered such combinations of tones? Suppose further that the composer of this series of chords admitted that what he had intended was to build a harmonic *crescendo*, in which the harmonic tension should increase sharply from the first chord to the fifth, followed by a *diminuendo* to the end. In accordance with our plan of leaving rhythm out of consideration, I have notated this example, too, in whole notes. This robs it, of course, of the slightest trace of attractiveness, and ruthlessly exposes the harmonic progressions in complete nudity. Let us now see whether the composer has succeeded in realizing what he intended.

The analysis of the five-voice example yields the following results:

1. *Linear construction.* Except for the next to the top voice, not one of the lines is built on sound principles of melodic construction. These principles are discussed in the next Chapter, and I shall

therefore leave this aspect of the matter for now with the assertion that the lines are poor.

2. *Two-voice framework*. No plan is apparent. Up to the fourth chord there might seem to be one, but the weak fourth g-c³ in the fifth chord flatly contradicts the intention to make this the harmonic climax; here a strong interval (fifth or third) would be needed, rather than an inversion, which (as we know from the combination tones) is lacking in energy. Chord 6, containing a seventh, should have been followed by a chord of lower tension. Instead, chord 7 contains the tritone, and even it is not resolved: it is followed by a seventh, and only this last interval finds a satisfactory resolution in the final fifth ab-eb².

3. *Harmonic fluctuation*. Obviously the composer had no conception of this. It follows an aimless, zigzag course which in no way results in the desired climax of harmonic tension in chord 5.

4. *Degree-progression*. The concentration of chords from the fourth to the eighth chord does not allow any harmonic life to unfold, while a further brake is provided by the repeated eb of the sixth and seventh chords.

5. *Guide-tones*. Their connection with the roots in the degree-progression is good, but they stand still in their tracks, and are accordingly, in this piece in which everything should contribute to the impression of movement, rather a hindrance than a connecting factor of repose.

6. *Tonality*. The tonal center in the degree-progression is undoubtedly G♯ (Ab), for that note occurs twice and is confirmed by the strong, repeated fifth. The leading tone, G, too, which occurs twice, strengthens the tonal center, and the third, B, also helps. In this connection the c♯ of the beginning and the A of the fourth chord are of subsidiary importance. The first four chords could also be related to A as a tonal center, supported by its third, c♯, and by its leading tone, G♯. In this case there would be a modulation from A to G♯. The tonal sphere of G♯ overlaps that of A, since it begins as early as the third chord; from this point on, the sway of G♯ is undisputed.

All in all, we can say that the composer has not solved his problem well. Let us help him to a better solution.

1. *Two-voice framework.* As in the original version, let the upper voice move in a broken line while the lower moves down stepwise:

But now the intervals are well arranged: the harmonically strong fifth is followed by the weak major sixth, then the strong major third, then the strong tension of the major second, resolving to another major third. Now the intended climax of the piece has the necessary support. The framework has its climax in the third chord, of which the fifth is only a lower and therefore weaker repetition. If we succeed in placing the harmonic climax at the fifth chord, by means of heightened tension, then the two-voice framework and the harmonic fluctuation will be at odds—a desirable result, since the opposition of forces enhances the life of the tonal texture. The weakest place in the two-voice framework is in chord 6 (except for the major sixth in chord 2), from which the return is made through the sharp minor seventh f♯-e² to the pure interval of the fifth.

2. *Harmonic fluctuation.* For the aimless arrangement of the fluctuation in the original version we shall substitute a planned distribution of the harmonic tensions. To accomplish this, several ways are open to us. If we wish to create the impression of a departure from rest and a return to rest, which would seem indicated by the design of the melody and the framework, we had better begin and end with chords of group I_1:

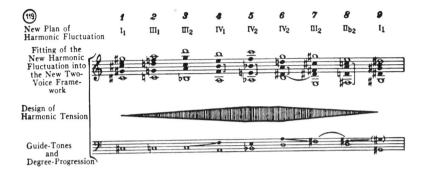

We can then place a chord of group IV₂ at the planned climax, and for the chords in between there will be several possibilities, of which those here proposed doubtless best serve the purpose. The reader is free to try other solutions. In filling up the chords we have a certain freedom in several places. We choose those solutions that make the best voice-leading for the inner voices. This produces the indicated form for our example.

3. *Degree-progression*. But we have produced a quite unusable degree-progression. The repeated c at the beginning and the broken chord formed by the roots of the fifth to the ninth chords are responsible for the unsatisfactory effect of the whole. We shall therefore make the following improvements:

and try to preserve the chord-scheme that fits the planned fluctuation. But this is not possible throughout, for in the seventh chord the new tone of the degree-progression, d, makes a tritone with the upper voice, and thus will always produce a chord of Group B.

4. *Guide-tones*. The line of the guide-tones is poor since, with the exception of·the first one (the f in the fourth chord), it contains nothing but the broken form of a chord of group IIb_1. The improvement of this defect would bring about the collapse of the whole structure that has cost us so much pains already, so we shall postpone it until we have treated the problem from the tonal standpoint.

5. *Tonality*. The tonal spheres are not clearly worked out. The skip of a fourth between the second and third tones of the degree-progression permits us to group the first tones, as far as the B♭, around c as a center, the c♯ at the beginning being taken as the upper leading tone of the c, unless one is to take it, since it is the first tone, as an independent tonal center. But as such it would lack any support. From the fourth to the eighth tones the center is B♭, the A as leading tone and the d as third being its auxiliaries, while the e♭, the fourth, appears as the neighbor of the harmonically stronger third. The tonal center G♯, which although it stands at the end and is reinforced by its upper leading tone A is not completely definite, would be stronger if we provided it with another supporting tone. This we can do by substituting for the d of the seventh chord, which stands a tritone away from the G♯ anyway, another G♯:

[162]

This note is a very strong (almost too strong) support for the tonic, being separated from the final note only by the A, which has now become a weak returning tone, and being itself supported by the dominant d♯ (e♭). This restores to us the possibility of placing a chord of group III_2 in the seventh place, as we had planned. But if we retain the IV_2 chord in the sixth place, the progression of the guide-tones will be poor. We had better therefore use a III_2 chord in this place, too; it will change the intensity of the harmonic fluctuation, to be sure, but not its direction. Indeed, we shall be realizing even better than before the composer's intention to make the fifth chord the climax. The line of the guide-tones is now just as correct as the degree-progression.

6. *Linear construction.* The voices which are not parts of the two-voice framework now have better lines than in the original version of the example. Complete purity of all the elements cannot be attained under the extraordinarily severe conditions which we set ourselves; the slight linear shortcomings at the end of the second and third voices are therefore to be regarded as the least of the possible evils.

I know the outcry that will greet such an analysis in some quarters: "Why, this is pure constructivism! What is there left for invention?" But it has always been true in the craft of composition that something which others had mastered and with which one was not yet thoroughly familiar oneself was looked on as invention-killing constructivism. The only reason the rules of harmony and counterpoint are not considered constructivist schemes is because we are used to them. Between these simple technical disciplines and a more comprehensive sort of instruction, where does constructivism begin? For him who has never thought about the theory of composition it begins no doubt with the first chords that he plucks like forbidden fruit from the tree of his insufficient harmonic knowledge; he loves them especially as the children of his sin against the theory of harmony, and consequently does not wish to know them in all their most hidden characteristics. But for the strong musician, who is sure of his creative impulse and of his knowledge, there is no

[163]

such thing as constructivism. Every additional device that helps him master his material brings him a step nearer the inmost shrine of music itself.

12

Non-Chord Tones

According to the procedure we have followed up to this point, we must consider every appearance or disappearance of a tone amid chord-structures as creating a new chord. This view is valid so long as the tempo is so slow that the alteration of the sound seems important enough to cause a separate chord to be perceived. But there are many such tones which do not produce independent chords—chord splinters, or offshoots, they might be called. Such tones enrich chords without essentially changing them. Melody, as we have earlier determined, is what sets tonal masses into motion. But melodic force works not only by a general attack on the inert chord-masses. It also splits off separate tones from the chords, in such a way that the ear perceives the new sound in the first instant as something exceptional and different from the ,normal run of chords, and relates it to the harmonic progression only when the next chord enters. The rigid chordal structure thus has to give up portions of itself bit by bit to melody, the action of which in these skirmishes is comparable to that of an acid upon a metal. A tiny bit of a mighty force gnaws and bites at the material under attack, not strongly enough to destroy it, and yet affecting the surface enough, by etching scratches and grooves into it, to roughen its smooth finish.

These little bits of melody strewn in among the harmonic texture have long been known as "non-harmonic" or "unessential" tones. I prefer the term "non-chord" tones. The following varieties may be distinguished: returning ("changing", "auxiliary") tones, passing tones, suspensions, neighboring tones ("appoggiature", "unprepared suspensions"), neighboring tones left by leap, neighboring tones approached by leap, anticipations, unaccented free tones, and accented **free** tones.

Returning tones. The returning tone occurs when one member of a chord moves from its place in the chord to another tone for a short time and then returns:

In most cases the new tone is a second above or below the chord-tone, but it may be further away. What is essential, however, is that the foreign tone should be less important rhythmically than the chord-tone—that is, that it should occur in a less stressed position. Usually it is at most equal to the preceding chord-tone in duration; a longer time-value would take away from its auxiliary character. Generally it is a tone really foreign to the chord—that is, the combination that occurs during the moment of its sounding belongs to a group of lower rank than the main chord. There are, however, returning tones that form a combination of higher harmonic value than the main chord, or that do not affect the value one way or the other. It is often doubtful whether such cases involve real returning tones or rather broken-chord formations.

Such returning tones usually occur in connection with chords of relatively low harmonic value, and they must be of short duration if the higher-value combination which they produce is not to usurp the principal place and so invert the intended effect. Returning tones may occur in more than one voice at a time:

and they may move in opposite directions:

[165]

There are also whole returning chords, in which the main chord is left for a new one, built on a different root, and then the main chord returns:

Here, too, it is often hard to decide whether the middle chord is only an auxiliary chord or whether there is a really significant change of chord and root. For the returning chord to appear unmistakably as such, it is even more important than for the returning tone that it should have the lesser rhythmic and harmonic value.

Passing tone. The passing-tone formation consists in a stepwise transition from one chord-tone to another:

It can consist of one tone or of several, and must, like the auxiliary tone, result in combinations of lower harmonic value than that of the main chord, and be of short duration and in unstressed position. Passing tones can also occur in more than one voice simultaneously, and in contrary motion:

But here there is the danger that the quantity and position of the passing tones will make them more important than the principal tones. Passing tones can also fill out the space between a chord-tone of one chord and a chord-tone of another:

In such cases the formation is not finished within the area of the

[166]

first chord, since the chord when it moves to the next contains the foreign tone; but the passing-tone character is preserved because the goal of the passing tone follows immediately in a new chord-tone or in the neighbor of such a tone. Auxiliary tones and passing tones also occur in two-part writing:

Here they produce an interval of lesser value between two intervals of greater harmonic or rhythmic importance.

Suspension. A suspension occurs when, in a succession of two intervals or chords, part of the first is held over into the second, where it creates a tension with the other chord-factors, and is accordingly resolved during the existence of the second interval or chord:

In two-part writing every interval can thus become a suspension which is subjected to the attraction of a harmonically stronger interval.

The most natural resolution of the tension generally occurs when the suspended tone moves downward by a major or a minor second. Upward resolution is good when it is by the step of a half-tone, because of the leading-tone effect, while upward resolution by step of a whole tone is less often successful.

The resolution of the suspension by the upward step of a major second is most useful when a leading-tone progression or several simultaneous half-tone steps in other voices contribute to the smoothness of effect.

In three or more parts the tension created by the suspension is greater, because of the greater definiteness of the surroundings; the effect of the suspension is accordingly enhanced, and the resolution is even more satisfying. We have established the fact that the suspension always resolves to a better chord-factor. But in three or more parts this does not mean that the chord-progression always follows the pattern poor—good. The effect of the resolution of a suspension is always created, even in writing in more than two parts, by the relaxation of the tension of a single interval. Thus in the three-part examples of Figure 131, the suspension—resolution relation is not always accompanied by the change from a sharper to a milder chord. Instead, the five chord-progressions given contain the following interval-successions, each embodying the principle suspension—resolution: minor seventh—major sixth; major seventh—minor seventh; major seventh—major sixth; major seventh—minor seventh; augmented prime (minor second, minor ninth)—major seventh. It should be noted that the ear places the succession suspension—resolution where it perceives the sharpest interval; in the first example of Figure 131, therefore, it hears it in the succession minor seventh—major sixth, and not in that of fourth—major third. For the same reason, the last example is felt to consist of the succession minor second—major seventh, not major sixth—fifth. Since the rhythm is determined by the chords bearing the suspension, the resolution usually occurs in less stressed position than the suspension: the reverse is infrequent. Suspensions can occur simultaneously in all voices but one, in any desired number, and resolving in different directions, even successively. But the ear will always seize upon one of them as the principal one, and this, as has been stated, will be the one embodying the greatest tension.

If the second of the two chords is one of the simpler varieties (that is, does not belong to groups III or IV), the whole first chord can be suspended, with the exception of one supporting tone.

Suspensions are not always resolved by step:

Often the tension may be resolved by substituting for the tone which would have been attained by step another good chord-factor; but this procedure is recommended only in very simple chord-relations. Between the suspended tone and its resolution, any number of tones may be interpolated, if they are so placed, rhythmically and harmonically, that they do not impair the effect of the resolution:

Particular warning must be given against tones which fit the chord too well, since they result in a premature dissipation of the tension of the suspension.

A particular variety of the suspension is the six-four chord before the dominant in the familiar cadence:

[169]

There is no reason to attribute independent value to it here, since it is entirely dependent on the chord that follows. In reckoning the degree-progression, too, it must be looked upon as a suspension, and thus has no root of its own but shares the root of its successor. The six-four chord in this usage has been called a "pseudo-consonance" or a "perceptual dissonance". In our system, however, chords cannot seem different from what they are, and contradictory interpretations of their degree of consonance cannot arise if their analytical assignment to the proper groups (I–VI) is rigorously carried through. When the six-four chord occurs otherwise than as the forerunner of the dominant, it keeps its own root.

A notion with which conventional harmonic theory seeks to explain those things for which it has no other place is that of the "unresolved suspension". Our system does away with this notion. The chord in which the alleged "unresolved suspension" occurs is an independent chord, belonging to one of the inferior chord-groups, and thus needs no resolution. The effect of tension and resolution created by the suspension may be found in any progression in which chords of inferior value are followed by those belonging to superior groups. Often only the rhythmic characteristics of a passage will indicate whether it contains a suspension or simply an undecorated chord-progression.

Unprepared suspension or neighboring tone. A tone occurring in a relatively strong rhythmic position, at the interval of a second above or below a chord-tone, and resolving to the latter while the rest of the chord remains,

may be considered a suspension without preparation or a passing tone which lacks the usual point of departure. It is particularly like a passing tone in effect when its step of a second is preceded by others, belonging either to chord-tones (of the preceding chord) or to passing tones:

[170]

Thus the very common scale-passages which are ordinarily viewed as series of accented and unaccented passing tones are really combinations of passing tones and neighboring tones, since our definition rejects the existence of accented passing tones. When the neighboring tone is relatively long, it has the character of a suspension rather than a passing tone:

This is true, too, when it is not weakened by being preceded by the step of a second, and is approached by leap instead:

Between it and the chord-tone that follows it, other tones may be interpolated, just as between the true suspension and its resolution, and what was said in the latter connection applies also here:

Neighboring tones, too, can occur in more than one voice at a time. Finally, a neighboring tone may be preceded by its own, subordinate neighboring tone.

Neighboring tone left by leap. On the final, rhythmically weak fraction of the time-value of a chord, one (rarely several simul-

[171]

taneously) of its tones may move up or down a second to a tone whose relation to the rest of the chord is less close than the original chord-tone:

Immediately following it, the new chord begins. The voice that has moved to the neighbor of one of the chord-tones of the first chord must reach its tone in the second chord by leap: hence its name. If there is no leap, the tone is only a passing tone.

Neighboring tone approached by leap. This is a tone (not often more than one at a time) standing at the interval of a second from one of the tones of the *second* chord, but sounding during the time-value of the first chord, which is what differentiates it from the unprepared suspension.

Rhythmically it must have slight value; otherwise it will acquire harmonic importance of its own. It must be approached by leap from the first chord. Like the neighboring tone left by leap, it must occur in a rhythmically weak position and be of short duration. Both of these types are inseparably connected with a leap; they differ in their relations to the chord-progression. The one is connected to the preceding chord, and the other to the following one. The characteristic leap *follows* the one and *precedes* the other.

Anticipation. This is the opposite of a suspension. One or more tones of the second chord of a progression are introduced too soon, so that they occur during the duration of the first chord:

The anticipation is as weak as the suspension is strong. The suspension increases the tension of waiting for what is coming, demands a certain energy for its understanding, and then rewards the listener

[172]

with the resolution. The anticipation is the premature satisfaction of the listener's curiosity, and it should consequently be handled, like a pleasant but very cloying flavor, with discretion. Since even one anticipation is apt to be very obtrusive, the simultaneous use of several anticipations is usually not advisable.

Unaccented free tone. A tone of slight rhythmic value, in unstressed position, which is not a part of either of the chords between which it occurs:

Its effect is similar to that of a neighboring tone approached by leap, but it is possessed of more tension, since it is not the neighbor of a chord-tone, but is approached and left by any interval not contained in the chords.

Accented free tone. This tone is in a rhythmically stressed position, and in this respect resembles the unprepared suspension.

But since, unlike that tone, it is not resolved by step of a second, but moves to a chord-tone by leap, it is sharper in effect, and does not create the effect of tension smoothly resolved.

There exists no convenient and space-saving set of symbols for the clear indication of the various kinds of non-chord tones in analysis. For this purpose we may use symbols consisting of letters to which slight additions are made to indicate their varying functions:

W Changing tone (returning tone) [*Wechselton*]
D Passing tone [*Durchgang*]
V Suspension [*Vorhalt*]
N Unprepared suspension (neighboring tone) [*Nebenton*]
N' Neighboring tone left by leap
N Neighboring tone approached by leap
V Anticipation [*Vorausnahme*]

[173]

F   Unaccented free tone

F   Accented free tone

(Note: The symbols of the original German text have been used in the translation. Where the letters used are different from those which would naturally be used in English, the German words from which they are derived are given in brackets.—*Tr.*)

Our discussion of the non-chord tones is based on the assumption of normal metric rhythm, in which the "strong beats" are stressed. When the opposite is true, in syncopation, the relations of the non-chord tones are correspondingly inverted. An unresolved suspension will then, since it normally occurs on the "strong" part of the beat, occur on the "weak" (but now stressed) part, and the neighboring tones approached and left by leap will occur at the ends of "strong" beats.

Among the non-chord tones the most varied combinations can occur: suspensions may be combined with passing tones, neighboring tones with changing tones and free tones. Moreover there are borderline cases in which it is not possible to label the non-chord tones precisely. Indeed it is often difficult to decide whether to consider a given tone as part of a chord or as a non-chord tone. What has been said above in connection with the suspension applies to all the non-chord tones. If the chords involved belong to groups I or II, then the explanation is simple, for the combinations produced by the non-chord tones stand so far below the main chords in our scale of values that there can be no doubt of their subordinate importance. But chords of groups III and IV are often just such combinations as are produced by non-chord tones with those of groups I and II. Value-differences between these chords and the still more complicated combinations they make with non-chord tones are hard to establish. If then the rhythm adds to the confusion, in that the added tones are not short enough to be unmistakably subordinate, a definite line cannot be drawn.

[174]

CHAPTER V

Melody

1

Theory of Melody

It is an astounding fàct that instruction in composition has never developed a theory of melody. Every student learns harmony, and from the traditional theoretical instruction one would think that the handling of tonal materials depended mainly on a knowledge of harmonic facts. But everyone knows that rhythm and melody form at least equally important parts of the musical structure, as well as that they are without doubt the more fundamental elements. The direct appeal to the senses made by a rhythmic succession and the curve of a melodic line are more easily remembered by the naive listener than the differences in tension between juxtaposed harmonies. The domain of harmony has been explored from end to end, while rhythm, as I have previously stated, has escaped all attempts to study it systematically. Melody, although no definite melodic theory has been developed, has not been entirely ignored in musical theory. The study of counterpoint begins with the building of the simplest melodies, and thus sets out from the first to complement the study of harmony. But unfortunately it does not follow up its first steps. Instead of a systematic investigation of melodic phenomena, instead of approaching musical writing from the standpoint of the movement of tones, it ends up in a more or less distinctive figuration of chord-successions constructed according to the rules of harmony. The results of this melodic research, which goes no further than its first steps, are embodied in the *cantus firmi,* of which the following is an example:

[175]

These brief melodic successions are still, owing to their firm structure and their cool impersonality, excellent types of primitive melodic formations (provided that they are well made and not just the mournful and characterless formulae of academic counterpoint), and they are useful even in music not of educational purpose as a basis for contrapuntal work, owing to these same characteristics. But what we mean in the usual sense by a melody is related to these primitive types about as one of the higher vertebrates is related to the star-fish. The melodies we know from the works of the masters are full of life, character, and independence.

It will not be maintained that free, living melody, one of the prime factors of music, is not important enough to be worth studying as a separate subject. The moment a student is advanced enough to begin what is called "free composition", melody, which has been neglected throughout his previous training, suddenly assumes its full importance. Now he is free to write melodies of the freest kind, and it is assumed that he is master of a craft of which he has been taught only the most elementary principles. Does the nature of melody somehow conflict with the strictness of theoretical instruction? Such instruction is only the road to a knowledge of the technique of composition. If it had grown so independent that it could consider free music, for which it is supposed to be a preparation, as a discipline which did not fit into its domain, then the time would have come to replace it with something better. Perhaps many people think that the forms of melody are too manifold and various to be summed up in rules. Yet they must have observed that the melodies of the masters are not built up without rhyme or reason. Anything made by man, no matter how many varieties it assumes, and how much of the superhuman it seems to contain, must reveal its secret to the close observer. Why should one not be able to analyze melody, when it is possible to reduce the incomparably more numerous and more ambiguous phenomena of harmony to a comparatively small body of rules?

There are grounds of another nature, I believe, which have kept theoretical instruction from including the systematic study of melody. Melody is the element in which the personal characteristics of the composer are most clearly and most obviously revealed. His creative fancy may hit upon the most individual harmonic progressions, the boldest rhythms, the most wonderful dynamic effects, the most brilliant instrumentation; but all that is relatively unimportant compared to his ability to invent convincing melodies. On this point the expert and the naive listener are agreed. Stylistic differences in melodic formation are often almost impossible to analyze. Several composers follow the same melodic line, and yet the version of each one is recognizable from the tiniest details. The material of harmony is enormously varied; it is not, however, critically sensitive. Melody, on the other hand, can be reduced to a few, meager, basic facts, upon which, to be sure, infinite variation is possible. Undoubtedly this possibility of variation is what made it seem hopeless to earlier theorists to set up a clear system of the laws governing tonal movement. There may also have been a certain hesitation about laying bare the most personal and secret characteristics of a composer. It was not hard to maintain this silence. For composers have seldom been good theorists, and when they have been, they have preferred to deal with the most elementary points, rather than with what really concerned them so closely, while other writers could hardly describe convincingly what they knew only from hearsay.

We shall not be undermining the nature of melody, of which the finest details will always elude analysis, if we seek to know the basic principles of linear movement. And in so doing we shall be contributing to the end of the arbitrary lawlessness which reigns in this department of composition, as well as to the clearing up of the obscurity that veils melodic questions in general. Perhaps after this fog has lifted only the short-sighted and the ill-willed will continue to speak of the want of melody in the music which at first seems strange, but of which the bold creators are no sooner dead than they are praised as the singers of divine melodies. Lack of rhythmic imagination and harmonic poverty are greater evils than inferior melody, and they are much more common. Yet one rarely hears them complained of. These fields are more familiar to the musician and the listener—rhythm because of its direct appeal, and harmony through habit and training; everybody understands more easily what the composer means, so far as these elements are concerned. Once the basic rules of melodic structure are as well known as the simplest practices of harmonic progression, judgements of melodies in a new and unfamiliar style will be more accurate than they have been.

2

Chordal Association

We simplified our study of the harmonic element of music by leaving rhythm so far as possible out of account. It will be useful to do the same in our search for the basic rules of melody. It may be objected that harmonic progressions are conceivable in which the influence of rhythm is reduced to the very minimum trace that cannot be eliminated in harmonic change, while melody is unthinkable without the continuous influence of rhythm. This is true. Every step from one tone to the next involves a duration relationship, and consequently depends on a regular metric beat as a unit of measure. Yet it is not at all impossible to disregard this simple influence of rhythm in our investigation. What is more difficult is to get along without rhythm as the regulator of forms, the connecting factor between time-units of unequal length. Even in the most primitive melodies, the tonal material falls into little pieces of unequal length: motives, for whose rhythmic construction the mere metric beat is no more sufficient than for the construction of larger formal units. If one is to construct melodies with the same sureness that is taken for granted in the setting up of chord-progressions, an exact knowledge of the higher elements of rhythm is indispensable. One should know as much about the form and inner dimensions of motives as about their number and duration. That we are usually satisfied with a more or less developed feeling of this part of melodic construction, instead of knowledge about it, is to be regretted, but, the field being unexplored as it is, understandable. Pleasant as it would

[178]

be to provide in connection with the present theory of tonal relations a key to the rhythmic part of our work, I must postpone the
solution of this problem to some later time. As an excuse rather than
as a justification for this shortcoming, I may point out that the
present theory thus stops at the same point as its predecessors.
Moreover, I am not writing a comprehensive treatise on composition, which would not be complete without an exact treatment of *all*
the elements of musical structure, but am only trying to introduce
law and order into the realm of the *handling of tones*.* The invention of melodies reaches beyond the knowledge that is needed for
the simple manipulation of tone, but the rules of melodic procedure
outlined in what follows suffice for the theoretical foundation of
the art of handling tones. So far as seems necessary for the creation of small melodic forms, the part of melodic work that has to
do with the construction of motives is discussed in the later volumes
of this work.

We have seen that in the harmonic progressions of a piece of
music not only the time-regulating force of rhythm but also forces
which regulate space and harmonic relations are operative. We have
become acquainted with the effect of harmonic fluctuation and of the
relations of the tones in regulating the harmony. We have also encountered the space-dividing energy of melody in the form of tonal
successions and of the two-voice framework, but we have had no
opportunity to examine the laws which govern these linear developments. These are what we must now investigate.

We shall start from the harmonic point of view, already familiar
to us. When we considered the fluctuation in harmonic progressions,
we tacitly assumed motion from chord to chord—a melodic phenomenon. Just as there a melodic force operated in the domain of
harmony, so harmonic force operates in melodic connections. We
have already established the fact that even when tones are sounded
successively, a root can be found among them. The connecting

* In the translation of the title of the original work, *Unterweisung im
Tonsatz*, the author was reluctant to see .the word *Tonsatz* (literally, the setting of tones) rendered by "composition", but diligent search failed to reveal
any fully satisfactory substitute.—Tr.

force of harmony is thus not confined to the tonal mass lying directly above the root of a chord, for it permits the root-predominance of one tone to be felt even in relation to tones sounding before or after it.

Root: $e\flat^1$

The most obvious form of harmonic connection in melodies is in the breaking of triads or the simplest seventh-chords. Melody of this sort cannot be very expressive, for it has hardly torn itself loose from harmony. On the other hand, it has something compellingly natural about it, which has always served to give the main structural points in a composition the mass and solidity which they require. We know this primitive kind of melody, still entirely dependent on harmonic forces, from the opening themes of hundreds of Classic and Romantic compositions. The symphonies, concertos, and chamber-music works from those of the early Mannheim school to those of Bruckner and Strauss would be unthinkable without this sort of lapidary theme construction. This type of melody shows clearly the fallacy of the idea generally entertained by music-lovers of romantic tendency that they wish to hear nothing but "beautiful" or even "expressive" melodies. The melodies we refer to are neither beautiful nor expressive. The openings of Beethoven's Fifth Symphony and of his C Minor Piano Concerto can hardly have overwhelmed a single listener in history with the beauty and loveliness of their melodic form. What is expressed in them is a will toward clear formal development: they are the counterpart to the harmonic cadence. In these thoroughly harmonic opening themes melody and harmony have *not yet* conquered the structural force of rhythm; in the cadence, form, having previously lost the upper hand to melodic and harmonic elements, regains it. If against such a harmonic and forcefully natural theme a second theme is contrasted, which exhibits in the most characteristic way the subtle charms of melodic detail, it is the juxtaposition of such different melodic types that permits the melodic structure of the second theme to be appreciated. This explains why so many composers of the post-Classic

[180]

period, despite the beauty and often even fascination of their thematic invention, fail to reach the heights attained by the Classic masters. They kill one beautiful theme with another, so that sharp thematic contrasts and consequent melodic tension are lacking— a lack which is brought all the more painfully to the attention of the listener by the faulty proportion between a content which is lacking in tension and a form which is of exaggerated duration.

If in a tone-succession based on a broken-chord formation there is an accumulation of non-chord tones, originating simply as decorations, the melodic element is brought more into the foreground and the harmonic element is subordinated. This process can go so far that in superficial listening one hardly notices any harmonic connection. But that such a connection is always present is proved by the fact that intervals have roots. The composer cannot do away with the harmonic connections of the intervals; but what he can do is to compress or spread out the melodic expanses over which these connections operate. A melodic line which, although it does not have the unfeeling massiveness of a mere broken-chord formation, still holds close to chords that hardly change, despite all its trimmings in the shape of non-chord tones,

will produce in the hearer a feeling of repose, or even, at worst, of boredom. On the other hand, frequent changes from one harmonically articulated melodic fragment to another produce a fresh, exciting effect, which can lead, if the roots change too frequently, to utter confusion, to a harmonic and melodic vertigo. The groups

[181]

of tones in a melody which are harmonically connected are like the links of a chain; they give the melody color and sheen. They are the real body of the melody, strange as it may seem to speak of body in connection with a linear phenomenon like a melody. It must not be forgotten that a melody is only *primarily* linear, and that the comparison with a curved line applies only to the most obvious, external aspect of a chain of tones. The melodic thread has an ever-changing but ever-present volume or thickness. How the outlines of this formation, which we have now recognized as having body, are drawn, we shall learn later.

There are extreme puritans who consider possible the construction of a melody without any harmonic connection. Although we know that this is not possible, let us demonstrate its impossibility just the same. If one were to connect only intervals of low harmonic value, such as minor and major seconds, still at some point a major or minor third in relation to one of the tones would be formed, which would give the whole group a harmonic sense. When thirds, or other intervals of strongly harmonic significance, occur directly, they draw the tones that surround them into their own orbits. With a combination of fourths, fifths, and major and minor seconds and sevenths it would be possible to construct a fairly extended succession which would not immediately reveal any inner harmonic connection. But this would only mean that the harmonic connection was not obvious, not that there was none. The power of fourths and fifths is so strong that they attract the entire attention to themselves. If several fourths or fifths occur in succession, the ear is made uncertain by the accumulation of clear harmonic groupings and their variety within a short space of time. The impression of lack of harmonic connection which such a passage gives is based, therefore, on an illusion—on a fatigue of the ear, actually—and not on any real lack of harmonic association. The ear is surfeited with harmonic groups, so that it can no longer follow them. But the harmonic center of such groups made up of successions of seconds, fourths, fifths, and sevenths within a melody can be found according to the given recipe, despite the frequent change of roots. Usually we do not have far to seek, for the ear tries, as we have seen, to discover a broken chord of groups I or II in every tone-succession. In broken forms of chords of groups III and IV, which is what successions of seconds, fourths, fifths, and sevenths make, it often finds hidden a simple triad, which it takes to be the skeleton of the succession. The other tones are then related to this triad as non-chord tones. Often it is satisfied with a single prominent interval—a conspicuously placed fifth, fourth, or third—to which it relates everything else as a melodic (*i.e.*, only secondarily harmonic) addition. But some harmonic connection the ear will always find—if not within two or three tones, then over a wider space. Consequently it is impossible to exclude chordal association as a factor in melody.

3

Melody Degree-Progression

The tone-groups contained in a melodic line are governed by the same laws that rule tonal combinations of primarily harmonic significance. Accordingly, everything that has been said about harmonic fluctuation and tonal relations applies to melodic groups also, although less strongly, since in them harmony is subordinated to melodic force. The effects of fluctuation, particularly, are obscured, since the ear always seeks triad formations in melodies, and usually succeeds in finding them in some form or other, by accounting for complicating factors as non-chord tones wherever possible. But the values of tonal relationships apply here with undiminished force.

The same device that enables us to establish the logic of a harmonic succession will serve us in good stead here; what tells whether the harmonic construction of a melody is logical and appropriate is the degree-progression. In order to set up the degree-progression of a melody, we shall enclose in a dotted bracket (see Figures 154—158) the notes which can be heard without effort as a harmonically related group. In general, these groups will form broken triads with non-chord tones. But often our analysis will yield more or less than a triad; less if a third or a fifth (or the inversion of one of them)

[183]

represents the only harmonic content; more if a chord of one of the inferior groups (III or IV) is easily to be heard. One hears the harmonic relations most clearly by playing a melody through slowly. When this is done, it develops that one cannot locate the beginning of a harmonic group until one is somewhere in the course of that group. The ear cannot hear what is going to happen. It relates each new impression to earlier ones. If a tone appears that could be the root of a group, everything which could easily belong to that group is related, retrospectively, to that tone. But perhaps it is immediately succeeded by another, which would form the root of a more comprehensive grouping. Then the new tone remains valid until the tones group themselves around still another. Thus if we have divided a melody into groups as follows:

we see that the harmonic groups are not always clearly separated from one another: they overlap, and at times smaller groups form parts of larger ones (see, for example, the end of Fig. 156). Often their outlines cannot be definitely drawn, and different observers will form different opinions about them. The more closely the groups interlock,

the clearer is the harmonic course of the melody. Of course, the

harmonic significance of melodic tones is dependent upon their
metric position. Rhythm, an even more brutal force than harmony,
exerts so powerful an influence that, for example, a chord of inferior
value, consisting of four different tones, appearing in broken form
in a stressed part of the measure, will rob triads which prevail
throughout the rest of the texture of much of their strength.

We now extract the roots of the harmonic groups of a melody
(or the root representatives, in indeterminate chordal groups) and
place them in succession, within the closest possible pitch-range. If
necessary, we can also complete the reckoning with the help of the
guide-tones that belong to chords of Group B.

We thus arrive at a series of tones that follows the rules we have
learned in connection with the degree-progression, i. e., whose con-

[185]

struction is mainly in accordance with the relationships of Series 1. Everything that we have said about the degree-progression—the best intervals to use, the things to avoid—applies here, too. The only difference is that this new degree-progression, drawn from the harmonic content of a melody, may show greater activity, and need not lean so heavily on the strong intervals—those near the beginning of Series 1.

One thing should be noted: the new degree-progression is complete in itself, and fully independent of the main degree-progression upon which the joint harmony of the several voices of a piece rests. In a piece made up of several simultaneous melodic parts, as many degree-progressions are possible as there are parts, and it is possible to imagine a case in which all these degree-progressions would be fully independent of one another. The independence of the melody degree-progression goes so far that the harmonic groups of the latter are in flat disagreement with the harmonic content of the whole piece or passage. The familiar theme from the Haydn "Surprise" Symphony

shows very clearly that against the dominant harmony of the whole (in the last measure) the melody degree-progression may show the tonic. The last measure, by virtue of its preponderance as the terminal point of this melody, as well as the f♯^{1} in the measure before the last, do indeed make possible a feeling of change toward the dominant, of modulation to G. But this is really true only for listeners who are not used to comprehending the melody degree-progression apart from the degree-progression of the whole. The listener who analyzes this melody precisely would require, for the assumption of a dominant or leading-tone effect, a d^1 (d^2) or a^1 in the melodic progression, in the absence of which the f♯^{1} is nothing but a neighboring tone approached by leap within a widely extended C₋major triad. Thus we see that it makes no difference to the melody degree-progression what harmony one imagines under

[186]

the melody. The only thing that counts is the actual harmonic content of the melody itself; this appears somewhat grotesque in an example like the foregoing, but in more complex constructions it will be found completely convincing. It would naturally be easy to read simple harmonies into the melody, agreeing with the harmony of the whole. But this would contradict an analysis that aims solely to show the *harmonic logic of a melody,* and does not seek to confirm in some other way what it has learned from the degree-progression of the entire harmony.

It often happens that the degree-progression of the harmony and the degree-progression of the melody are in full agreement. This results in a fine, straightforward, but sometimes insignificant clarity. Just as often, the two progressions are opposed. How wide the gap between them may be, whether they coincide except in certain details or go their own brutally independent ways—these are questions that can be settled only by experience and taste, not by technique. No one will want to go so far as to say that nowadays the best result is always attained through opposed degree-progressions. Unquestionably even the little-trained listener can tolerate independent progressions more easily than in former days, but it is still sensible to produce strong harmonic tensions only when the style and purpose of a piece demand it. Nothing is gained by attaining the contrast of the degree-progressions at the expense of the effect of the whole—that is, by setting a well-developed melody to harmonies that completely contradict it, just for the sake of this contrast.

4

Seconds

The real building units of melody are seconds. They perform two functions in melodic space, just as in harmony the harmonic intervals perform two functions (that of the fluctuation, and that of tonal relation). The influence of the fluctuation is felt in the slightest change of a chord, while the effect of the relationships requires greater extension in space. Similarly, steps of a second in melody act on the one hand as the measuring units and content of the briefest melodic sections, and on the other—like the relationships in harmony—as regulators of the larger melodic connections.

They are used to fill out the harmonically stronger intervals, but they are also placed immediately before the first tone of such an interval or after the second one. Often they produce simply non-chord tones (N, V, N', N, etc.), as when the harmony belonging to the main tone does not change with their appearance. But if one of their tones is an essential part of an independent chord, they are no mere melodic decorations but become important structural members of both the harmony and the melody. As in the cases of all melodic intervals, the direction in which a second moves is of the greatest importance to the form and effect of the melodic curve.

The step from a higher tone to a lower is always felt as a relaxation of tension. This motion is undoubtedly the most natural one in music, since the production of a higher tone requires, at least in all instruments in which mechanism does not play a large part, greater energy than that of a lower one, and accordingly a step downwards gives the impression of diminished resistance, of an approach to rest and to the end. The singer, whose instrument is more sensitive than any other to the differences in tension between tones of different pitch, feels this most clearly. But even keyboard instruments, which on account of their mechanism should give the listener the impression that it makes no difference whether one moves up or down, or over how great a distance, do not entirely conceal the feeling of lessened resistance in a downward movement. What other explanation is there for the fact that the very common downward interval of a fifth from the dominant to the tonic, which occurs in the bass in the commonest of all cadences, is felt, irrespective of instrumental questions, as a fall, and even explicitly as a final fall?

The downward interval is, because of its tendency to a decline and resolution of all tension, sterile: nothing grows out of it. In a rising interval, the energy of the performer gathers impulse, and the fact that a certain space has to be traversed and a certain physical resistance overcome frees that energy, and exercises an effect of gathering excitement and tension on the listener. The larger the interval, the greater this effect—particularly, again, in singing, or on instruments which show the necessity for additional physical and mental energy more easily than do the keyboard instruments.

The melodic principle that a rising interval creates tension and a falling interval resolves it is affected by the harmonic tendency to connect different tones. If, for example, the rising or falling interval takes place within a single chord, so that both tones of the interval are members of the same chord, there is no feeling of either rising or falling tension. Even wide leaps are of little effect in these circumstances. The distances here spanned have been marked out already by the presence of the stationary chord, even if the ear has not counted the second tone of the interval as belonging to the chord until this tone actually appears. Consequently, the traversing of this space involves no effort, and it does not produce in the listener the feeling of expectation fulfilled that he gets when the leap is made to a non-chord tone, or when it is accompanied by a change of chord.

It would be impossible to sum up all the possible melodic intervals within our system; it would even lead too far if we were to try to examine the characteristics of every upward and downward interval within the octave. Accordingly, we shall confine ourselves to the space of a fifth. In the wider intervals either we see an intensification of the relations that govern those below the fifth, or else the larger intervals are split up so that there occur in detail the same phenomena that we shall observe among the thirds and fourths. We limit ourselves further to the investigation of falling intervals. If we wish to know the effect of the rising ones, we need only change the minus sign in our result to a plus sign. We shall keep carefully in mind the fact that the effect of a melodic interval is strongly influenced by the rhythm. The normal results, which we shall arrive at by *disregarding* rhythm, will thus in practice be subject to change according to the time-values and metric positions of the tones concerned.

The succession e(e♭)-d-c, the most common of all downward melodic divisions of the third,

brings the e(e♭) into relation with the c, according to Series 2. But the d, acting as axis, balances the forces to the extent of preventing the weight from falling suddenly and heavily on one side. The e(e♭) retains a certain part of its independence. Not so, however, if we substitute a d♭ for the d:

The leading-tone tendency of this tone makes the c so strong that the e(e♭), now abandoned to its fate, becomes the mere vassal of the c. In the succession e-e♭-c,

the connection with the c is just as strong. Since the third appears in two forms, and the step from the major to a minor third represents a decline in value, according to Series 2, it loses its original power and cannot resist the root-power of the c. The succession e♭(d♯)-e-c embodies a rise in value:

but the relation to the c is still very strong, since the e♭(d♯) has the effect of a neighboring tone of the superior major third, and thus loses its independence. The same is true in lesser degree in the succession d-e(e♭)-c.

In the successions d♭-e-c and d♭-e♭-c, the d♭ has the effect of a neighboring tone of c, with the e or e♭ interpolated between it and its resolution. In all these cases, the e or the e♭ is subordinate to the c. Thus we see that there is no purely melodic way to purge the interval of a third, however it occurs, of its harmonic value. To diminish that value, rhythm must be called upon.

In the following example we see the fourth divided up into three intervals:

The f is hardly more than a neighboring tone of the third e-c or e♭-c; the last four successions can also be looked on as pairs of thirds, which would yield the degree-progression d-c or d♭-c. If the fourth is to be independent, the third must be subordinated by rhythmic means, or omitted altogether. In the successions f-d-c and f-d♭-c, the fourth predominates:

but one must be careful to give the d or the d♭ slight rhythmic value, since otherwise the third f-d or f-d♭ will come to the fore, and produce again the degree-progression d(d♭)-c. The successions d-f-c and d♭-f-c

also permit the fourth to prevail, if the d or the d♭ has slight duration. The third becomes almost completely harmless if it is used exclusively to reinforce the fourth, as a neighboring tone before it:

The division of the tritone by seconds presents no problems. We remember the description of its characteristics in Chapter III, according to which it must always occur either in chordal grouping or in subordinate melodic function (as a neighboring tone).

The division of the fifth into a series of descending seconds always gives the effect of a triad with varying emphasis upon its different factors. The succession g-f-e . . . c

[191]

makes the third, e, prominent, while g-f♯-e . . . c stresses the fifth more, because the f♯ is tied by the half-tone to the g; the same contrast exists in even sharper form between g-f-e♭ . . . c and g-f♯-e♭ . . . c:

In g-e-e♭ . . . c, the e♭ is important, because the diminution of value between the two thirds makes the e sound like the neighboring tone of the e♭. In the successions g-e-f . . . c and g-e♭-f . . . c

the fifth is liable to sacrifice its value by becoming part of the third e-g (e♭-g) or the neighboring tone of the fourth. If the fifth is to be prominent, it is provided with a neighboring tone (f-g . . . c, f♯-g . . . c, a♭-g . . . c, a-g . . . c):

If, on the other hand, the root is to be emphasized, then it is preceded by a neighboring tone d-g . . . c, d♭-g . . . c).

If the entire interval of the fifth is traversed in minor seconds, then all these fine differences of tension are destroyed:

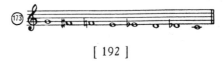

[192]

Accordingly, division of the fifth by chromatic seconds has the lowest value.

Familiarity with the system briefly sketched here for the smaller intervals must be gained through practice and experience. The recipe given will then make it possible, if it is felt desirable, to reckon the effects of seconds in the division of other intervals within the octave. But, combined with experience, a healthy musical instinct will be a more reliable guide through the innumerable possibilities of interval-succession than the most careful reckoning.

5

Step-Progression

Important though the detailed work of seconds as connecting links between the harmonically significant tones of a melody may be, they achieve a really dominant position when they become the guide-posts of the melody. As such they regulate its horizontal and vertical extension, and are thus the complement of the degree-progression, which is the guiding line for its chordal coherence.

Every melody consists of prominent tones and subordinate ones. On the one hand, the roots of the little chord-groups in the melody —that is, of the "body" of the melody—must be considered the more prominent tones. Their chief function is the setting up of the degree-progression, and as the regulators of the degree-progression they have had their just evaluation. But within a melody there are other main tones whose significance is *primarily melodic*. Among these may be the roots of the chordal groups which are the pearls on the string of the melody, but more important are those tones which are placed at important positions in the two-dimensional structure of the melody: the highest tones, the lowest tones, and tones that stand out particularly because of their metric position or for other reasons. The primary law of melodic construction is that a smooth and convincing melodic outline is achieved only when these important points form a progression in seconds. The line that connects one high point to the next, one low point to the next, and one rhythmically prominent tone to the next, without taking into consideration the less important parts of the melody lying between these points, is called the *step-progression*. It is easy to draw. If we play a melody through slowly, and listen carefully to the points that mark the pitch limits, the step-progression separates itself almost without any effort on our part from the rest of the melody:

Melodies of simple construction exhibit a simple step-progression. In such melodies, the step-progression consists of a single succession of upward and downward steps of major and minor seconds, to which we need merely make certain subordinate additions toward the construction of further step-progressions. The more complicated the structure of a melody, the greater the accumulation of hidden harmonic groupings in it, the greater its compass, the richer the mixture of larger and smaller melodic intervals—the greater the number of step-progressions will be. Thus in a well-constructed melody there may be four or more step-progressions going along simultaneously:

Every one of them may be independent of the next, and without any connection to it. But that is not necessary. Step-progressions may be many or few, and may be fully independent or may pass from one into the other. The less stiff and forced their development, the smoother and clearer will be the course of the melody. A useful function in this connection is performed, outside the step-progressions, by tones which do not move, but repeat themselves at short intervals and prevent the interplay of the step-progressions from leading to an over-rich and confusing development. (See the encircled notes in Fig. 174.) The distance in time from one of the prominent melodic points that forms a step-progression to the next cannot be stated in a rule. The tones forming a step-progression are sometimes in direct succession and sometimes widely separated.

Like everything else, the construction of step-progressions can be overdone. A barren creeping up and down, with the high and low points mostly occurring in close succession, destroys in the listener any feeling of tension, such as he derives from observing a step-progression which does not always move just as he expects it to.

In the step-progression, octave transposition may take place, so that sevenths and ninths may replace seconds.

This occurs in melodies in which the space of one or more octaves is filled out with chord-groups of strong harmonic coherence. The cohesive power of the broken chord is such that the connection of a tone in one octave with a tone in another is at once clear. In fact a melody full of leaps, even without such chordal organization, invites octave transpositions in the step-progression; but such melodies are not very common.

There are exceptional cases in which the progress of a melody does not take place according to our rule of seconds. This happens especially when a melody moves quickly from one register to another by means of a broken chord in either an upward or a downward direction.

[195]

Here, too, the harmonic stability of the broken chord assures the coherence of the whole, no matter whether the tone that stands outside the series of seconds is a third, a fourth, or even further distant. Finally, the prominent tones of a melody may not belong to either a chord or a step-progression,

when the need for intense expression requires that the attention shall be riveted by the conspicuous strangeness of such tones.

If clearly perceptible broken chords can burst the confines of the space outlined by step-progressions, it follows that step-progressions may conflict with melody degree-progressions. The harmony that is implicit in the melody—the harmonic flowering, so to speak, of the degree-progression—may assume such importance that the setting up of a step-progression becomes unnecessary. In a type of melody which does not go beyond chordal factors and shows scarcely any linear development, the degree-progression is thus the only regulator of melodic growth. If, however, the chordal groups of such a melody permit the erection of a step-progression, the latter enjoys greater freedom than ordinarily: it may contain sharp interruptions, breaking off at one place in a chord and beginning again at another, without obscuring the meaning of such passages.

6

Conclusion

We have arrived at the end of our reflections on the structure of melody. What services do the melody degree-progression and the step-progression render the composer?

They are indispensable for the analysis of existing melodies, in which one always begins with the determination of the harmonic content as the cruder ingredient, extracting the degree-progression and then seeking for step-progressions. It will be found that there are pleasant, attractive melodies of which the degree-progression is satisfying, but of which the step-progression is faulty, either because of its monotony and lack of the elements of tension and surprise, or because of its planless construction:

d'Albert, Tiefland

Step-Progression

Such melodies give listeners no more than a certain pleasant impression. Other melodies, especially those which strive for the most definitely linear character, may have a well worked-out step-progression and a poor degree-progression. Such melodies make the listener restless, since he can follow the vague harmonic connections only with difficulty. Balanced and well-rounded melodies, on the other hand, which give the listener a sense of joyful well-being,

Beethoven, 5th Symphony

Degree-Progression

etc.

exhibit a beautiful equilibrium of the two progressions. The succession of harmonic formations is convincing because it rests upon a logically developed degree-progression, while the line of the melody carries the listener securely to the desired points because the clear step-progressions do not allow him to wander from the path. And the two kinds of progression are so constructed that they do not conflict.

But in the work of construction as well as in that of analysis the reckoning of degree- and step-progressions is of help to the composer. How often it happens that a theme which is based on a good idea will not assume the form which the composer would like to give it! He tries this and that, but there remain passages which he cannot seem to perfect either by the help of a better melodic idea or by the most conscientious polishing. If these passages are good in themselves, they do not fit the rest of the melody. Or the general outline of the melody is good but the details are poor. To find out what makes the tones so refractory, he need only apply the measures of degree-progression and step-progression. He will learn either from the degree-progression that a poor harmonic succession is obstructing the course of his melody, or from the step-progression that there are holes in his melody—leaps or vague connections that prevent it from growing as it should. If he then changes the tones at

[198]

these particular places in such a way as to improve his degree- and step-progressions, his theme will suddenly take on more convincing form.

An example will explain this procedure more clearly. Suppose a composer had invented the following melody:

This melody may appeal to some and not to others, but let us completely disregard judgements which depend purely on personal taste: a melody such as this may be encountered often enough nowadays. We have, to be sure, torn it away from its context. We do not know its exact purpose. It is possible that it might have a particular task to fulfill for which it must have just this form; but that is not probable. Judged as a melody, this series of tones is poor. The degree-progression is not good because the tritone-chord formation e-b♭-f♯ makes too strongly coherent a section at the beginning. The latter part of the degree-progression is usable, although one may question whether so much space should be devoted to the harmonic center g, which dominates the section from the second to the seventh tone, and whether the strongly harmonic grouping b-g-e-c♯ (6th to 9th tones) should be retained. Only slight suggestions of step-progressions are present. They are not sufficient to give the hearer the feeling of reliable melodic guidance. If now we improve the degree-progression in such manner (we need not go into the individual steps of the process here; they are illustrated in Book II) that it acquires the following form,

[199]

and if we build some step-progressions into the structure (the method of doing so here employed is only one of many possible ones), we shall achieve a melody that uses the same motives as the original one, but that is indisputably better constructed from both melodic and harmonic points of view, and is accordingly more convincing.

Degree-Progression

There is a notion, springing from ignorance of the working-processes of the artist, that the true artist can be as "wrong" as he likes; that if he does something "wrong" it makes sense and is better than much that would be "right". This notion assumes the presence of a special guardian angel that permits liberties in artistic work which are not granted in the other domains of human endeavor (not without their own importance!). According to this idea, composing, writing, and painting would be ideal occupations for all sorts of know-nothings, and one would have to pity those who sullied their fresh, unspoiled point of view with comprehensive technical knowledge. But things are not as simple as that. What is "wrong" in the usual sense is so only with reference to inadequate theories of composition, which apply a narrow measure to the abilities of a composer. But no one can devise and write things which are "wrong" according to the principles of the step- and degree-progressions if he wishes to make his music as intelligible as possible to his listeners. It will not be denied that the theory here put forward is more comprehensive than its predecessors; and any trial will show that it applies just as well to any style of the past as to the music of our own time. The objection that the musicians of the past had no idea of these progressions and yet were great masters is no objection, really; on the contrary, it is the best proof of the natural foundation of this system. If there are composers even today who know how to handle all the tonal materials unerringly without knowledge of the precepts laid down here—yet without simply imitating wiser men—they are to be praised and envied. But others will welcome the help here offered them. If on the other hand, a man lacking in talent attempts to rely entirely on such knowledge, without having any real gift for his work, the most perfect working out of step- and degree-progressions will not help him. Everything he does will be correct, and yet we would gladly do without it. There have always been many rules of the craft, and now come more. When one has mastered them to the extent of being able to use them with the same facility as one uses older precepts, one will find that one has taken a significant step in the direction of clear and wholly satisfactory writing. But no one will be so stupid as to assume that what has been impossible throughout all ages is now possible: to create a work of art without creative impulse, simply by burrowing and calculating.

CHAPTER VI

Analyses

The following examples and their analytical dissections are intended to show that the music of all styles and periods may be analyzed by the methods proposed in this book. The advantages which these methods offer the composer in his creative work cannot, alas, be displayed with the same ease. They may be observed only in one's own work along the lines here suggested; for such work, the practical books of this series will outline the necessary training.

Having read the foregoing chapters, the reader should have no difficulty in studying and appraising the following analyses. Often he will arrive at different results from those here given. There is no harm in that. I have in each instance chosen only one of many possibilities. Moreover, the notation of a piece of music is the mere chemical precipitate of the work itself. The charm of the latter lies not in scientific exactitude, but in the fact that it arouses in the hearer not alone direct emotional enjoyment, but also a pleasure in the recognition and judgement of the impressions received. Even with the closest familiarity with the objective content of a work of art, the judgements of all observers will never completely coincide.

In the musical examples, the harmonic relations are indicated by the addition of the symbols for the non-chord tones. By eliminating the latter, the harmonic fluctuation and the degree-progression are calculated. In the degree-progressions, the guide-tones are included in such manner that the step from the root of a tritone-free chord to the guide-tone, and vice versa, is indicated with a line leading from one to the other. If for reasons of voice-leading the guide-

[202]

tone has to approach or leave the octave of the root of a tritone-free
chord, instead of the root itself, the octave is included in parentheses.

1. Dies irae — Melodic Analysis

It may seem strange to apply our analytical method to music of
which neither the theory nor the practice have ever yielded to attempts of this sort. Yet no one will deny that in these most linear
of all compositions chord-groups are hidden, whether with or without the intention of their creators. The search for the logic of these
groups justifies us in setting up the degree-progression. The plot-
ting of the step-progression will surely meet with no objection.

Ⓐ Melodic Analysis

1   Main Voice

2   Degree-Progression

3   Step-Progression

Ⓑ Harmonic Analysis

4   Two-Voice Framework

5   Fluctuation

6   Degree-Progression

7   Tonality

The principal voice (the second from the top), which in the original is provided with words, is, with its stepwise motion only occasionally interrupted by leaps, so centered around the tone c^1, that in its degree-progression the strong harmonic steps of the fourth and fifth alternate in the pleasantest balance with the strongly melodic seconds and the chordal thirds. The step-progression seems at first glance a little sparse. Closer inspection shows, however, that the oft-repeated step of a second d^1-c^1, with its intensification e^1-d^1 (in the tenth and eleventh measures) is based on wise calculation. The melody is thus set in motion only gradually, while in its later development (not given in the quoted passage) it is elaborated with a considerable variety of motives, and in the refrain it reaches full bloom. We thus see included in the step-progression an artistic device which in general is a hindrance to melodic development (the frequent repetition of two tones), here justified by the purpose of the whole structure.

No one will wish to measure the melody of this early music with the same yardstick as our modern melodies, pregnant with expression as they are. It is extraordinarily simple, and at the same time leaves the greatest possible room for *harmonic* development. The latter is not expressed in the arrangement of the degrees: the degree-progression of the complete harmony is limited to the establishing of c as the tonal center, by means of sure and unhesitating steps, with emphasis on the subdominant, then a modulation to f, and a return to c. But the conflicts of detail between harmony and melody, above this firm foundation, are worthy of the highest admiration. There are the boldest oblique accumulations of non-chord tones, as well as parallel fifths, sevenths, and seconds—all features which can only today again be felt as correct and beautiful, because we again have the ability, common in Machaut's time, to separate harmonic and melodic elements while listening, and to weigh one against the other. We see in this music a true counterpart of the Gothic style of architecture of the same period, in which the great, central features of the structure are of elementary simplicity, corresponding to the harmony of this Ballade, while the fullness of decorative detail, here represented by the non-chord tones, is almost oppressive.

The *harmonic fluctuation* made up by the principal chords is hardly noticeable in the maze of decorative lines, and it consists only of the very slight value-differences between chords of groups I_1 and I_2. The *two-voice framework* shows most clearly the connection of this music with that of later times. It is very subtly constructed, with the intervals cleverly distributed. Observe the feeling of rest produced by the parallel octaves in the fifth and sixth measures, making the sharp cadence, with its parallel ninths, the more prominent. The same effect is seen at the end of the example, where the repose induced by the octave e-e[1] in measures 13 and 14 is interrupted by the last two quarters of measure 14, forming the cadence, this time with the very intense parallel motion in sevenths.

* During a rest, the tone preceding the rest must always be regarded as remaining part of the harmony, for the rest interrupts only its actual duration and not its harmonic significance.

This piece is a true Chinese puzzle, from the harmonic point of view. The ear is constantly offered a choice of what it wishes to hear: independent chords, or subordinate, non-chord tones. Only by the latter can formations as striking, in a style of simple tonal relations, as the a-chord in the f minor (or c minor) of the fourth measure, and other similar places in the course of the piece, be explained. This intentional uncertainty goes so far that even in the first measure, in which there are only two voices, the listener does not know exactly what is meant. When he follows the design of the upper voice, he is inclined to hear the highest tone of the three-tone motive as a neighboring tone, and the third tone (g^1 and a^1 in the first measure) as its resolution. But the presence of the lower voice shifts the effect of suspension to the fourth eighth-note (though this suspension does not have its full effect, since a condition favorable to it—the placing of the interval of stronger tension in the stronger metric position—is not fulfilled). And it makes the last eighth-note of the measure a returning tone, which on the first eighth of the next measure, despite the rest, becomes a suspension. In the third measure, however, the relations originally expected occur, and the third and seventh eighth-notes can really be heard as neighboring tones. In the seventh measure, the listener has to change his interpretation again, and so it goes throughout the piece.

It is quite possible in listening to sum up the harmonic content as consisting of fewer chords of longer duration, which would result in an even greater number of non-chord tones. Thus the degree-progression for the third and fourth measures would be:

and for the ninth and tenth:

The harmonic fluctuation shows clearly the uncertainty in which the listener is placed. Except for the series of intervals in the first measure all belonging to group I, there is an uninterrupted succession of waves. The differences in tension between the chords are very small; only rarely does the tension rise above group II. (Chords of group VI do not indicate any sudden rise in tension: their indeterminate quality makes them adapt themselves to their context, and produce hardly any more tension than those of group II.) It is the very active degree-progression that creates the necessary tension. Consider how the tonal relations of the center F are exploited in measures 5–9. The ambiguity of the chordal texture, the continual swing of the pendulum back and forth between chords of little difference in tension, and the degree-progression worked out with every resource of tonal relationship—all these are unified by the great repose and purposefulness of the *tonal structure*. The tonalities succeed each other almost exclusively by steps from one center to another closely related one. The constant, restless flux of all the structural elements that can be directly heard rests upon broad and firm harmonic foundations. The contrast between the harmonic stability of the background and the nervous unrest of the chordal content is one of the greatest charms of the piece.

The *two-voice framework* partakes of the active nature of the foreground. It corresponds exactly to the two outside voices at any given moment, is easy to follow, and is accordingly not notated separately here.

4. Richard Wagner
Tristan und Isolde, Prelude

Melodic Analysis { Degree-Progression, Step-Progression

The Prelude to *Tristan* is one of the finest examples of the elaboration of a two-voice framework. The observer of the intervals formed by the outside lines of the harmony will be astonished to see how intervals of varying tension are juxtaposed. The procedure is illustrated beginning with the very first chord: the interval of a minor third (written as an augmented second) is followed by a major third, which represents a decrease of tension; the tension is then sharply increased again in the tritone on the first eighth of the third measure, only to be resolved completely in the fifth which follows. In this admirable way the tensional development of the framework is calculated from beginning to end, as the section here notated illustrates.

No less remarkable is the handling of the *harmonic fluctuation* and of the *degree-progression*. The distribution of the harmonic tension produces a beautifully varied succession of sharp and mild chords—chords of Group A and chords of Group B. Yet this ebb and flow dispenses almost entirely with chords of the highest tension—those of group IV. In the degree-progression, both the roots and the guide-tones are admirably treated. The first measure with its up-beat is treated as a broken chord, because the ear relates the two tones; likewise the fifth, eighth, and ninth measures. In measure 9, the d¹ of measure 8 has to be taken into account, and thus beneath the a¹ of measure 9 there is a root, d¹. The six-four chord in measure 18 is so passing in character that one is justified in taking its bass tone as its root, just as in a six-four chord preceding the dominant in a cadence. The same is true in measure 32.

In the analysis of the *tonality* it should be noticed that those roots upon which tritone chords are built must be regarded as dominants of tonics lying a fifth below. Thus the tonal center of the first three measures is a, and of measures 5–7, c. If we set out the centers of the various tonalities in succession, we obtain the following series:

from which it appears, in view of the repetitions of A and its support by its most closely related tones, that A is indisputably the tonal center of the whole; and this is still further confirmed in the later development of the piece.

One cannot expect, in so wonderfully constructed a harmonic organism, to find an equal perfection of melody. It is impossible to balance the two elements exactly; one of them must always predominate. Here melody yields first place to harmony. It confines itself for the most part to steps of a second and broken-chord formations. Thus nothing remarkable in the way of either melody degree-progression or step-progression can arise. The continual stepwise motion yields too little harmonic result for the degree-progression, and this stepwise motion is itself the step-progression, which is not built on large lines. But in the place where melody assumes somewhat greater importance (measures 25–32) I have added the melodic analysis.

5. Igor Stravinsky, Piano Sonata 1924, 1st Movement   Harmonic Analysis

The analysis of the opening of this work produces such simple results that it seems unnecessary to add any explanation. The tonal construction is revealed by the degree-progression. It is a broadly developed group around c as a center. Since this one tone dominates the entire section quoted, it is not notated in the example.

6. Arnold Schönberg, Klavierstück, Op. 33ª (Measures 19-29) Harmonic Analysis

After the foregoing analyses, the dissection of the example on pages 217–218 should also be clear. The reader is now in a position to appraise the harmonic fluctuation, the two-voice framework, the degree-progression, and the tonal scheme without further guidance. To make the analysis of the chordal relations clearer, I have reproduced the piece, immediately below the original notation, in the version which results from the ear's gathering together of the units of broken-chord formations and delayed sections of chords and its exclusion of non-chord tones from the harmonic combinations. I have analyzed the piece only from the *harmonic* point of view because the melodic element seems to me to have retreated far into the background in this piece. Those who disagree are free to undertake the melodic analysis for themselves. The tonal ordering of this fragment springs from the desire to group in the analysis as many chords as possible around one tonal center, so far as that is possible at all in this case. Subdivision of the longer sections would result in shorter and frequently changing groups, which would perhaps reveal the harmonic content of the example better than the tonal analysis given here.

It will be objected that no analysis of the present sort was in the mind of the composer when he wrote this piece. Although this objection applies to all music, since this type of analysis has never been in use before, let the piece be divided, in order to illuminate the viewpoint of the technique according to which it was written, into the sections into which it falls by the rules of the twelve-tone system. These sections are indicated by roman numerals, and bounded by dotted lines. In almost every one of them, all the twelve tones are conscientiously included, although obviously individual tones may be repeated. So far as I am able to judge this technique, group II seems to have been badly slighted, for it must get along without the tones e♭, f, a♭, and b♭.

7. Paul Hindemith, Mathis der Maler, Prelude

A Melodic Analysis of the Upper Voice.(the other moving parts can be dissected in similar fashion)

1 Degree-Progression

2 Step-Progression

B Harmonic Analysis

3 Two-Voice Framework

4 Fluctuation

5 Degree-Progression

6 Tonality

*) The organ-point is disregarded in the analysis

The strongly chordal design of the degree-progression is based upon the effort to organize chord-groups as closely as possible around a tonal center, while leaving the greatest freedom to the individual voices. The fact that the tones of the degree-progression (measures 9–13) form a broken chord of group VI results in a gentle but very noticeable cadencing toward the B of measures 13–16. The tonal scheme shows the same effort. Here, too, a large group of tonal centers is chordally related, so that great activity of details takes place against a smooth and gently restful background. At three points in the example there are organ-points. The first and last of these are left out of the reckoning. If one includes them, the degree-progression becomes simpler, but the harmonic fluctuation more complicated, while the harmonic construction is unchanged. In the second case (measures 9–12) the exclusion of the stationary c simplifies the reckoning; and here, too, the harmonic picture is unchanged.